In Search of the Meaning of Life (

GW01216588

Book Nine - England, Scotland, Wale

~~~~~~~~~~

By

Mark D. Jones

(Copyright 1994, Mark D. Jones, All Rights Reserved)

~~~~~~~~~~

Book Cover Photo Credit

I took this photo of my bike in front of the Eiffel Tower during my adventure in 1979 and it's one of my favorites. I love the symbolism of the dove flying by in the photo representing freedom to me. While my adventure into France didn't go according to plan due to my not speaking French, I love France and have since visited the country and Paris many times over the years!

~~~~~~~~~~

To Esther and David

Preface

It had been my dream for years to bicycle through England, Scotland, Wales and France, and even beyond if I could find a way to tour the entire Continent. It was now the spring of 1979 and I was finally planning the adventure I'd always dreamed of taking! It was like a waking dream that I couldn't believe was not only happening, but coming true right before my eyes. Ever since I was a kid reading books about knights and castles, I'd wanted to visit the British Isles and see Old World Europe, as it was a place my heart had always longed to visit.

Bicycling overseas was the logical extension for me following the 8,111 mile bicycle adventure my friend Bruce and I had taken around the United States in 1976-1977, but actually achieving this dream of traveling overseas was harder to accomplish than even I had thought it would be. Everything in life was expensive and tickets to Europe didn't grow on trees, so for the longest time I thought my dream was out of my reach and not possible. I wasn't born with a silver spoon and didn't have a trust fund to finance my dreams, yet I'd nurtured my dreams growing up in our Midwestern suburbia and was determined to one day make them my reality.

My friend Bruce returned to Michigan following the end of our journey around the United States I called *The Great Adventure* and I was on my own in the beautiful Emerald City of Seattle on the shores of Puget Sound. I did my best to put my time there in Seattle to good use, working my way up the ladder at Electricraft Stereo Centers, Inc. and loved working in the world of high-fidelity audio equipment, but ultimately I wanted to live an adventurous life and see the world.

While I'd experienced a multitude of adventures during my two years living in the Pacific Northwest, from adventuring to the bottom of the Grand Canyon to the heights of climbing mountains, flying a hot air balloon and getting a hands-on lesson in fixed wing aviation, I still had a difficult time trying to achieve the adventurous lifestyle I'd always dreamed of living. I'd actually committed myself to living a life of adventure and was now struggling as to how to find a way to make it happen.

I'd originally wanted to become a veterinarian since about the sixth grade and initially thought it was my lifelong dream, but later realized it was only an extemporaneous dream of trying to live the life of Dr. James Herriot in the wonderful stories about the rural veterinarian in North Yorkshire I'd read about and watched religiously through the book and TV series *All Creatures Great and Small.* My older brother had wanted to become a doctor and achieved his goal, so it only seemed logical growing up that I'd decide to be a veterinarian because of the unconditional love I'd felt through animals.

It was only after not being accepted into the College of Veterinary Medicine at Michigan State University in early 1976, that I later understood what I really wanted in life was to live a life of adventure. I still admired veterinarians and loved animals, but the entire field of adventure provided me with a much wider scope of options to choose from and Dr. Herriot's lifestyle in North Yorkshire was but one example of a life that had captivated me. My only problem at the time was answering the question of how to live a life of adventure without having the means necessary to finance it.

At the time, I didn't really have a purpose anymore at MSU as I had no idea what type of degree would actually work for me and decided to leave college until I understood why I should be there in the first place. I had committed myself to living a life of adventure in my dorm room on the sixth floor of West Wilson Hall in the early spring of 1976, without really understanding how I'd actually be able to pull it off. It's always one thing to say you'll do something, but it's quite another to go beyond words and follow through with it. Talk is cheap, as the saying goes. I'd gone beyond the point of just saying the words though. I'd actually committed myself to myself in terms of staying true to this spirit of adventure of mine and now needed to find a way to pull it off.

It took an entire summer of working my second year as a seasonal Marine Patrol Sheriff Deputy patrolling the lakes of Genesee County, Michigan, as part of the Search and Rescue SCUBA Diving Team, to save enough money to embark on this initial bicycle adventure with my friend Bruce. He worked with me patrolling the lakes of Genesee County, and as preparing for our adventure was expensive in terms of the bikes and equipment we'd need, we each ended up leaving home with less than $500.00 to journey around the United States with - but we'd done it.

The problem now, as I was living on my own up in the Great Northwest, was to find a way to replicate such a feat beyond just taking weekend trips and annual vacations, but it wasn't easy to figure out. I wanted to experience more than just short-term excursions - I wanted to take epic adventures!

After two years of living and working in the retail audio business in Seattle, my status quo had grown pretty comfortable for me and I liked everything about my life at the time. I'd climbed the corporate ladder so to speak at Electricraft Stereo from warehouseman, warehouse manager, merchandise coordinator and finally to assistant general manager for the new stereo stores the company had acquired in Idaho and Montana, and my job had given me plenty of adventure along the way in the process.

I'd taken the *Road Trip of All Road Trips* around the entire Western United States with another guy at the company, hiked to the bottom of the Grand Canyon, backpacked in Olympic National Park, experienced the Pacific Coast from Los Angeles to the Olympic Mountains, visited many of the prominent National Parks across the Western United States, climbed deep into the Teton Mountains and scaled Lone Peak at Big Sky Resort, MT, and traveled most every road and highway back and forth numerous times between Seattle and Billings, Montana - and even lived in a company apartment in Billings for a couple of months.

However, the crux of the problem was that my job had turned me into a nomad on the road driving an old box truck full of stereo gear beyond my normal rotation between Seattle, Southcenter, Bellevue and Lynnwood, WA, to my new stomping grounds of Boise and Pocatello, ID, and Bozeman and Billings, MT, for up to 72 days at a stretch. I was living this extended life on the road and wasn't happy with how my future appeared to be shaping up.

I had flown in our company's new hot air balloon I nicknamed *Miss Electricraft* for an entire summer now and experienced a little informal instruction in a twin-engine turboprop charter flying to Boise and back, and these new experiences had taken my adventurous spirit to new heights. My life was full of adventure, so what was the problem? How had I failed to live up to my pledge to myself to live a life of adventure? The issue was simply that the fun was gone...

I liked my life in Seattle and living the life of a nomad on the road didn't agree with me. I liked Billings enough, but didn't want to move there. I loved Bozeman, but didn't have the opportunity to take full advantage of it while living out of a suitcase in hotels in the dead of winter. I wanted to remain in Seattle and figure out how to live this adventurous life, because the audio business and our huge blowout warehouse sales had run their course, and I didn't want to be doing that for the rest of my life - so what was the answer?

Not only was life in general and in Seattle in particular an expensive proposition, but even thinking about traveling overseas seemed to be beyond my abilities and expectations. I couldn't afford such a trip - not now or ever it seemed. I'd always wanted to take a follow-on adventure to bicycle around the British Isles and venture across to the Continent, but that was simply pie in the sky thinking at the time. My dreams were too large for my limited ability to carry them out it seemed - not because my spirit of adventure was too weak, but because my financial means to carry them out was almost nonexistent.

However, adventure knows where it belongs and found a way to creep into my life without my even knowing it, until the answers were as clear as the nose on my face when looking into the mirror. When there's a will there's a way, as the saying goes. My odyssey as a nomad traveling the highways of Washington State, Idaho and Montana became a disruptive force at the time, and served a major purpose in my life.

The entire concept of adventure is geared towards finding ways to shake us, wake us, rattle our cages and remove us from the death grip of the status quo that's strangling our will to do anything else in life. For it is the process of sinking up to our necks in the quicksand of the status quo that entraps and immobilizes us from making decisions, acting on our plans and following through with our intentions of turning our hopes, dreams, passions and desires in life into our reality.

It was only through the disruptive force of adventure while traveling down lonely roads and highways, that I was able to be taken to my desert place to see life from an entirely new and different perspective. I didn't have the status quo distracting me at every turn and enticing me to remain within its steely grip of cozy comfort, but instead I was agitated, uncomfortable, lost, alone, abandoned, discarded and isolated in an old beat up box truck with stacks and stacks of audio gear traveling to far flung places that took me away from the status quo.

The last thing the status quo wants to see is for adventure to approach anywhere near it, for even an unhappy experience in the realm of adventure serves to remove us from the status quo and possibly kick it to the curb of life. Adventure is the antithesis of the status quo and the one thing it fears the most, as it exists only to prevent itself from being replaced and discarded.

Adventure is like a predator that eats the status quo for lunch. It steals us away to new heights and new opportunities where we can see the world through new eyes to live our hopes, dreams, passions and desires in life. Adventure gives us time to think - really think - about life and the life we've been living. It reminds us of our hopes and dreams. Nothing kills hopes and dreams like the status quo, squishing and squashing the life out of them while we binge watch TV and eat junk food on the couch.

Adventure equals action, and status quo equates to inaction and lethargy in the equation of life, and it was adventure - even a disquieting adventure - that spirited me away to my desert place to think quietly about life and more importantly about my life in particular. It took me away on a sabbatical so to speak where I wrote a book of philosophy and saw clearly for the first time in a long time the road ahead of me into my future. I couldn't see beyond the far bend in the path up ahead, but the straight stretch in front of me disappearing into the fog was still crystal clear - I was to follow my heart, and live my hopes and dreams!

I realized I'd always wanted to bicycle overseas and see the world, and if I didn't make this trip now I'd regret it for the rest of my life. Nothing really mattered to me beyond the logistics of adventuring overseas, and I knew I was taking a calculated risk to give up and strip away all I'd achieved over the past two years for all I might become, with no promise of success for either the trip or my future.

In fact, adventures are always geared towards failure anyway by definition, as it introduces so many random variables, elements, risks and pure chaos into the equation that the default option is always to fail - never to succeed. Like mountains eroding into the sea, everything in life degrades and breaks down over time, not the other way around to rebuild and regenerate itself into a higher order. I knew I'd have to be the one element in my adventure equation to somehow survive the journey and figure out how to rescue it from ruin. It would be a difficult task I knew, as I'd never traveled outside of the United States before and only spoke English.

However, adventure knew I was wrong in the way I was thinking. While I would be a major part of the process of trying to make this new adventure a success, much of it wouldn't be up to me at all. As with much of my life since leaving MSU in the spring of 1976 to attempt to live a life of adventure, it had been others who had stepped up to the plate to take care of us during *The Great*

Adventure - complete strangers at the time who actually made the real difference.

It had been complete strangers who assisted us during our adventure of over 8,000 miles around the United States during our journey in 1976-1977, and it was also other people who helped me land on my feet in Seattle. Of course, I had to do my part on this next adventure as I'd always had to do in the past, but the real make it or break it determining factor on my trip overseas would be the warmth, hospitality, generosity and graciousness of complete strangers. For it was people I'd never met before, who would not only make the difference in helping me out during my trip, but would be in fact real lifesavers and blessings to me - and for that I'm forever grateful!

In order to make this trip happen on a shoestring budget I had to resign my position at Electricraft, sell my MG BGT, use most of my savings to buy gear and get my bike into touring condition again, buy my overseas ticket on a Pan Am 747 with enough in reserve to pay for my open return ticket home, and purchase traveler's checks for the actual trip itself. I started with $1,000.00 in traveler's checks while getting ready for my adventure and decided to leave a separate $500.00 behind in my bank account in Seattle in order to have a few pennies once I returned home after the trip - all the money I had in total. This was all a tremendous risk and a gamble, throwing away all I was and had achieved for the promise of an adventure, with no way of knowing if it would work out or be worth it in the end.

Regardless of the success or failure of my upcoming adventure, I'd inevitably return to Seattle homeless, jobless, carless and broke, so it seemed like I was setting myself up for complete failure either way it went. I didn't care though, as I knew if I didn't embark on this solo-bicycle adventure through England, Scotland, Wales and France - and perhaps beyond - then I'd regret it for the rest of my life.

I'd just have to sort out what to do once I returned to Seattle and somehow find a way to land on my feet again before I turned into someone homeless living on the streets. My heart told me this was what it wanted me to do and if I'd learned anything in life, I was sure that one of the most important truisms concerning meaning and purpose in life was to remain true to who we know ourselves to be - it's originally finding out for ourselves what our calling in life really is and who we are as a person, that can be the most difficult part.

I'd learned over time, and through trial and error, that I was filled with a spirit of adventure and needed to remain true to who I knew myself to be. It was this truth that allowed me to pursue my hopes and dreams of seeing the world, and let the chips fall where they might in dealing with the aftereffects of my decision. I was committed to follow this spirit of adventure and once I made my decision to leave Electricraft Stereo and bicycle overseas, I never looked back! Cheers! Mark

~~~~~~~~~~

Introduction

This is the story of the first part of my solo-bicycle adventure to England, Scotland, Wales and France, where I gave up all that I was in Seattle at the time in May 1979 to follow my heart for the uncertain promise of becoming all I could be. All I knew at the time was when I returned to Seattle I'd be homeless, jobless, carless and pretty close to penniless, but it was that important to me to remain true to my spirit of adventure and honor my commitment to myself to live a life of adventure, and somehow make all my hopes, dreams, passions and desires in life come true.

I'd already fulfilled one dream of mine to bicycle 8,111 miles around the United States on an epic journey I called *The Great Adventure* with my friend Bruce during 1976-1977 and the question I needed to answer to myself was whether I could do it again. Was it important enough to me to escape the comfort and empty security of the status quo to follow my heart, and if it was, was I up to the task of enduring another adventure? Adventures are never easy after all and they bring risk, random events, chaos, uncertainty and more right into the center of one's life - was I ready to handle it all over again?

It's the comfort and empty promises of the status quo after all that results in hopes and dreams withering away on the vine, dying a slow and agonizing death from the lack of care, attention, nourishment and nurturing required to keep them alive. Our passions and desires turn to dust and blow away in the winds of a parched and lonely desert in the same manner, if not watered and protected each day of our lives. Our idyllic childhood aspirations for our lives - as well as our grownup ambitions to be more, do more and live more - can get choked out by the brambles of life that entangle them within the false narrative and comfort of the status quo until they no longer receive the sunlight they need to thrive.

Such is the graveyard of life's hopes and dreams that go unfulfilled in life when their caretakers simply give up on them. I had committed myself to living a life of adventure when I left Michigan State University in the spring of 1976 to bicycle around the United States to both find myself and discover the country I lived in. I didn't want to live a life of regret having given up on my dreams of travel, so I stripped away all I was at the time for the chance of becoming so much more.

Once I made my decision to resign my position at Electricraft Stereo Centers, Inc. as assistant general manager for our audio store subsidiary in Idaho and Montana, and sold my MG BGT and began disentangling my life to undertake my bicycle adventure overseas, the same old feelings of questioning my abilities and sanity came nagging back into my mind. What was I doing? I'd be homeless, jobless, carless and penniless on my return to Seattle, with nothing to go back to and nothing in Michigan to return to either. Was I crazy? My mind couldn't comprehend this unraveling of the life I'd built in Seattle over the previous two years.

However, my heart rejoiced with the news I'd be following my longtime dream of bicycling through the U.K. and Europe, as I'd always wanted to see the Old World ever since I was a kid reading books about knights, castles, legends and lore, kingdoms and empires. This was my opportunity to follow my dreams and it was my heart's excitement in making this decision that assured me it was indeed the direction I needed to take in life. This narrow, overgrown, seldom-trod and less-traveled by path in life was the only direction my heart longed to take, and the direction my life needed to travel down.

I've split this journey of mine overseas into two parts, because my adventure really had two separate elements to it - the first part was a tour of Southern England with a dash to the Continent looking for sunshine that failed miserably. The second half of my adventure was a tour of Scotland, Northern and Central England, and Wales as my money began running out, to the point of needing to make sure I had enough money remaining to return to London Heathrow by train if needed, to fly home on a Pan Am 747.

In both cases, I was treated like a long-lost family member by the people of the British Isles with such warmth, hospitality and graciousness that it in-and-of-itself is the heart of my story. At the same time, I endured such physical challenges during each half of the journey that I thought would literally break me. Yet I survived and ultimately thrived in this green and pleasant land that I've always loved across the Atlantic.

While a good portion of my film and photos from this journey were ruined by the X-Ray machines in customs (I didn't know at the time to hand carry my film canisters through customs), two of my very best photographs did survive and are used for the book covers of each half of this adventure. The first, the photo of my bike in front of the Eiffel Tower is used for the cover of this *Part One,* and the other of my bike in front of the beautiful meadows, fields and hedgerows somewhere in the English countryside will be used for the cover of *Part Two.*

My hope in publishing these two volumes is that somehow the people who helped and assisted me on this adventure of mine, or their children, will come to know how very much I appreciated their help and assistance in the successful outcome of my trip. Over the past years and decades my life's been so busy and chaotic, and full of adventures following adventures, that I was never able to keep in contact with everyone I'd met on all my travels, so these two books are essentially my long-overdue thank you letter to all of them for all they did for me in the late spring and early summer of 1979.

After preparing for my trip overseas, purchasing the equipment I needed and getting my bike ready to go, I had only $1,500 dollars to my name. I left $500.00 in my account in Seattle to have available when I came home and set aside $1,000 for actually taking the adventure. After paying $36 for additional supplies prior to departing and $207 for my initial flight on Pan Am to London Heathrow, I had $757 remaining. I knew my open return ticket to fly home would later cost me around $202.00 (actual cost) in the U.K., which meant I only had $555.00 in traveler's checks available for the trip itself.

I'd just have to make do with that amount while overseas and make the trip last as long as I could. I had no concept of how far my money would last, as everything was a guestimate in my mind as to how much I'd spend each day. I'd originally wanted to be gone at least six months, but if things didn't work out I might not last two weeks.

In essence, $555 for my journey overseas wouldn't go very far and was, in fact, even less if I wanted some money left on me in reserve so I wouldn't be penniless on my departure date, say $100. A realistic amount of $455 in spending money while overseas wouldn't take me very far in the U.K. and on the Continent, but I couldn't do anything about it now and would have to stretch it as far as I could. Once I'd purchased my departure ticket in the U.K., I would be focused on making sure I'd be able to return to London Heathrow to make my flight. Everything in-between was simply an attempt to stretch my time overseas as long as possible before having to pack up and go home.

It turned out that in the process of compiling the details of my overseas adventure for these two books, I hadn't recorded all the details of my day-to-day spending in my logbook. Towards the end when I was bicycling back down from Scotland towards Berkhamsted in Southern England, I recorded an entry where I didn't even have enough money left to purchase a train ticket to London Heathrow if I'd had to in order to make my flight home.

That entry told me I'd been spending much more on my journey than I'd actually recorded in my logbook, yet I couldn't adjust any of the daily spending amounts as I don't know when and where I actually spent the extra money. So in *Part Two,* I'll make a large adjustment to indicate the unrecorded money I'd spent that never got written down, so as to account for how much the trip actually cost me. In the end, I'd have almost no money on me as I flew back to Seattle...

The real lesson learned from my journey was that if everyday folks in the British Isles hadn't helped me out by giving me a place to sleep and camp on their property, and fed and invited me into their homes, my travels would have had a completely different outcome - especially if Evon, the purser for the ferry company taking me across the English Channel for the second, third and fourth time hadn't gone the extra mile to find my missing bicycle for me. Had these events gone the other way, I would have been in a very difficult situation with little money or options to choose from and failed miserably on this journey I'd embarked on. Fortunately enough for me, it was through the kindness of complete strangers who'd taken it upon themselves to welcome me into their homes, treat me like family and help me along the way that saved the day and the trip for me - not anything I did on my own.

So here I was overseas in the British Isles trying to make the best go I could of the situation and the rain, having no idea what to expect when the time came to return to Seattle. The truth was that nothing was waiting for me there on my return, as I'd resigned my position and given everything up for the hopes of completing this adventure. On top of that, there was nothing waiting for me back in Michigan either, after dropping out and leaving Michigan State University in the spring of 1976. In the back of my mind I had no concept of what my life would look like on my return home, nor knew what I'd possibly be able to do about it. I didn't like to think about it during the time I was overseas, but from time to time it crept into my awareness causing me self-doubt as to the sanity of my decision - especially while immersed in cold, freezing rain, and the times I felt lost and stranded on the road.

It was this inspirational knowledge that regular folks and complete strangers were taking care of me on the road far from home that overrode my fears though, as I knew something very special was happening. In fact, it was similar to how Bruce and I had been taken care of while bicycling around the United States. It was this knowledge and awareness that I was being taken care of on the road by complete strangers, which set aside my fears of nothing awaiting me on my return to Seattle, as I understood I couldn't do anything about it in advance and simply had to deal with it once I flew home. The fact that I'd never not been taken care of in life before, gave me a quiet reassurance and confidence that somehow I'd find my way and my future, and be provided for again.

There is no experience in the world quite like being completely exhausted, wet and cold out there on the road and having a complete stranger offer to take you into their home, provide you with shelter and the comfort of a warm bed, bath and a meal. It makes the human experience we all share deeply personal and touches your heart in appreciation for their decision to care for you. That feeling and knowledge alone was a priceless gift given to me for all I'd experienced during my adventure that I'll forever be grateful for!

While I didn't know it at the time, once I returned to Seattle I'd find myself spontaneously embarking on brand new adventures I'd never even contemplated taking before, as the risk, randomness and chaos of my new situation completely changed the old parameters of my life. I was off to new destinations on journeys that seemed impossible just days and weeks before, while at the same time, taking me to distant places I'd never dreamed of visiting before. These adventures would try me both physically and mentally to the point of my succeeding and failing along the way, while the kindness of complete strangers would again astound me with their hospitality, openness and graciousness. This was yet another lesson teaching me about the real priorities in life, a lesson that couldn't have been taught to me in any other way than in my graduate studies in *The School of Hard Knocks.*

This story now travels down two separate pathways, as *Part One* begins to follow along with my logbook as it records my thoughts and planning process in Seattle leading up to my departure for London Heathrow, U.K., before continuing the account of my travels through Southern England and my excursion into France. As with all my adventure logbooks, I first display my logbook account for the day it was written, which more often than not requires a certain amount of literary interpretation to polish it up from the tired and weary account at the end of a day's adventuring into a format suitable for storytelling.

Secondly, I introduce 2018 Editorial Comments on most days following my logbook accounts, in order to provide additional background material about what I was thinking and feeling at the time, along with additional experiences I'd taken part in beyond the actual written entry I'd made in the logbook. Despite all these passing years, I still recall most of these details very vividly, especially the ones that have really sunk deep into my memory, as these experiences were the products of my hopes and lifelong dreams being realized!

So here we go, traveling 39 years back in time, as my logbook begins to tell the tale of this amazing bicycle adventure I took through the idyllic countryside, town centers and capital cities of England, Scotland, Wales and France!

~~~~~~~~~~

Table of Contents

~~~~~~~~~~

Chapter One - Planning, Preparing & Pondering

~~~~~~~~~~~

May 1979

~~~~~~~~~~~

I planned to depart on my solo-bicycle adventure to England towards the end of May 1979, so after I returned to Seattle by Greyhound Bus earlier in the month after attending my older brother's wedding in Detroit, much of my remaining time was spent in planning and preparing for this new adventure. In the days leading up to my departure date I applied for and received my passport, resigned my position at Electricraft Stereo on May 7th, sold my beloved MG BGT back to the dealer I originally purchased it from, stored my things in the basement of Jim's house, and prepared my bicycle and equipment for the journey across the pond.

I was getting excited to begin this new adventure and as a way of introduction to it I'll start at the beginning. I called the original 8,111 mile bicycle adventure I took with my friend Bruce around the United States in 1976-1977 *The Great Adventure* - and my logbook for this new solo adventure of mine to England begins with my excitement of attempting to find a name to call this new overseas adventure.

I was still wet behind the ears and had much to learn about myself and the world I was preparing to visit, so my focus in naming this new adventure was a tad bit misplaced - but it clearly illustrates the mindset I held at the time - with the entire world of possibilities for my future just waiting for me somewhere beyond the horizon. So my logbook begins with the following entries as I grasped for a way to define this new chapter of my life:

~~~~~~~~~~

There and Back Again

or...

The Search for the Grail

or...

The Quest for Adventure

or...

The Ultimate Journey

or...

How I Rode My Way to Fame and Fortune

I like that one the best...

~~~~~~~~~~

In the end while preparing this manuscript I decided to simply call this: *Book Nine - England, Scotland, Wales and France (Part One).* This journey would be my first overseas trip and my initial introduction to the many countries around the world I'd visit during the course of the rest of my life. I would find once again on this journey that people would care for me in the most amazing ways during my visits with them, just as they had around the United States on *The Great Adventure.* I was slowly learning through *The School of Hard Knocks* and life experience that the focus of my life should be on other people and God, not myself, which was a very difficult lesson for any young adventurer to learn.

I would keep relearning the same lessons in life until the concept finally sank in that my life wasn't about me, but about the many lessons I'd learned while traveling the wandering pathways of my life. The fact that people have taken care of me wherever I've traveled in life - well beyond these early adventures of mine - demonstrates the fact that at the center of my life are the lessons I've learned, which are a reflection of this care and concern that has been extended to me over the course of the many adventures of my life.

This new bicycle adventure was simply a continuation of a bigger lesson plan that my life had been immersed in for years. Somehow God was instructing me through the extraordinary kindness of complete strangers to release my pride and focus instead on the greater world around me. This realization would later lead me to join the United States Air Force in the fall of 1981 to live a life of service as a navigator flying jets for a twenty year career. So as I continued my preparations for this new adventure in the spring of 1979, I was actually preparing for the adventure that would be the rest of my life...

~~~~~~~~~~

2018 Editorial Comment: This was such a stimulating and exciting time for me as I prepared to embark on this new adventure that would really take me on the journey of the rest of my life. I had no idea of anything else at the time, except for the day by day plans and preparations I was making to get ready for this overseas trip. I couldn't have told you much about the future except for the fact that I was following my heart and spirit of adventure to finally travel overseas to begin seeing the world.

There was no way to know if this trip would succeed or fail, or what I'd find, if anything, on my return to Seattle. I couldn't have even told you how long I expected to remain overseas, as I could only hope for a longer trip versus a shorter trip, but that was the best guess I could make. I wouldn't have much money to spend on the actual adventure itself and would have to rely on folks helping me out and assisting me on my travels, but beyond hoping to get refills for my water bottles and a place to camp on someone's farm, I had no expectations that anyone would help me at all. On all of my adventures, I've never asked more than a polite request to have my water bottles refilled, for directions and/or if I could pitch my tent or camp out in someone's barn for the night to get out of the weather.

I was traveling on hope at the end of the day, as without some sort of baseline assistance of water and a place to camp, this would be a very short adventure indeed if I had to pay for places to stay. Did people travel around the U.K. and simply ask to camp on farms along the way? I had no idea. I didn't even know if people would be friendly, let alone offer to help me.

Everything was up in the air, causing me a certain amount of trepidation I tried to ignore in the days leading up to my departure date. There was only one way to find out of course, which was to simply fly to London Heathrow on a Pan Am 747 and get started on my adventure. I'd either find a way to make this bicycle trip work out or I wouldn't. After all, the proof is in the pudding, as they say. As it turned out, I wasn't the determining factor in how my journey would turn out at all, for it was out of my hands and in the hands of complete strangers...

~~~~~~~~~~

Jim's House, Queen Anne Hill, Seattle, WA

~~~~~~~~~

My Logbook Begins...

Tuesday, May 22, 1979

~~~~~~~~~

Well, it all begins again. I leave one week from today, on Tuesday, May 29th. I'll depart Seattle at 6:30 p.m. Seattle time and arrive at London Heathrow at 11:30 a.m. London time on Wednesday, May 30th. I believe I finally have everything I need for the trip, but I'm sure to find something that I've forgotten. I picked up my last paycheck today from Electricraft and I'll bring $1,000 with me and leave $500 here at home in my savings account. It really is very hard to become completely debt free, as I finally am now. Every time you turn around there's another bill to pay or hand in your pocket it seems.

I have tensed up a bit in these last few days. My first few unemployed days were great and I was in the best of spirits, but then I began spending a lot of money on bills and equipment. At least I have the very best equipment for the trip. I learned long ago that if you scrimp by on the equipment, then you had better not even take the adventure.

My mom's pen pal in England said they won't be able to pick me up at Heathrow when I arrive, and it worries me that my money is running out already and the high prices over there won't let me stay very long. I hope the trip doesn't fall apart after six weeks or so. On the way back to Seattle I'll probably get stuck in New York, and then have to find my way to Michigan and then back to Seattle. What if it all happens in the wintertime?

When I arrive in London it should be a real treat trying to put my bike together at Heathrow after the long flight and then not have a clue as to where I am. The underlying question I have is whether or not my experience of staying with other people in the U.S. will work in the U.K. and/or Europe? If not, it could be a very tough and expensive trip. I want to see how far I can stretch the money I've got and make it last.

But enough of all these problems! A trip is not worth taking if there aren't obstacles to overcome. If it was going to be easy, then anyone could do it and I wouldn't have accomplished anything great. Our previous bicycle adventure turned out just fine and I've done very well for myself in Seattle, so I have no doubts whatsoever that I'll make this trip work out somehow as well. When I get back from the U.K./Europe I'll tackle the next hurdles, but for now I must concentrate on this trip.

Well, I'm strong and in good shape. I've dropped five pounds since returning to Seattle from Billings and I've been walking all over this city to get my legs back in shape. I've got a tremendous tan started, the bike's in good shape and I've got the best equipment possible - so no problem! I worked a little on my comic strip today, drawing some preliminary sketches. That's about it for today, tomorrow I'll continue writing. I should keep a log everyday - adventure or not - it would be interesting reading in my old age.

~~~~~~~~~~

<u>2018 Editorial Comment</u>: I was experiencing such mixed feelings one week from my departure date as I wrote this account. One moment I was worried about all the details that seemed problematic at the time and difficult to overcome, yet in the next, I was positive and optimistic again. It's hard to remain positive when facing an unknown future, as our minds can vacillate between good and bad outcomes as easily as we can think about anything else. It takes real focus and concentration to remain positive and optimistic not knowing how things will turn out, but it has to be done.

At the same time, we might say that being overly optimistic in view of uncertain odds is foolish, as the laws of probability and chance alone tell us that no one can predict positive outcomes 100% of the time, so it's smart to hedge our bets and take some time to examine negative possibilities. However, without knowing what the future holds, much of that examination turns out to be just worrying, which does us no good at all. While normally a very positive and optimistic person by nature, I can fall into self-doubt and worrying just like the next guy, which after all, only makes us human.

I found the trick to overcome such negativity is to simply remain focused on the things that are within your control. As you take care of those details, you remain focused on only the actual conditions you can affect and not the unknown ghosts of the future that can take up residence in your mind. In this way, it's through the actions of preparation more than anything else that are the true indicators of future success, for it's all about the details. The more details you get right before leaving the starting gate, the higher the chance and probability you'll also get future details right as well. Past performance, after all, is the greatest predictor of future success, as it's all in the details.

Another point I'd like to expand on here in the opening pages of my logbook, is this comment I made at the very end. It was a revelation of sorts to me as I wrote the remark, "*I should keep a log everyday - adventure or not - it would be interesting reading in my old age.*" This is particularly telling, in that I'm now self-publishing all my early adventures in life at the age of 62 and relying on all the notes, clippings, photos, logbooks and written drafts I've kept over the course of much of my life.

While I never did take to journaling on a daily basis, I was aware that my adventures and experiences were unique, and one day I might want to write them all down as a way to preserve them. I would go on to bring a logbook or lined yellow legal pad with me on most of my travels from this point on, taking notes about each day in logbook form. During my time back at Michigan State University from 1980-1981, I wrote down my memories of living in Seattle to record my life there while they still remained fresh in my mind. For all the gaps and details in-between my scribbles, notes, clippings, photos and writings, I've been able to research many of them so as to reinforce, fill-in, date, verify and substantiate my memories and early writings based on the events and happenings back in the day.

Over the decades of my life, one of my major concerns was trying to make sure I'd never lose this hardcopy collection of scribblings, notes, clippings, photos, writings and early typed drafts I'd accumulated during the age before computers. I've collected binders of material from my early days that if lost, would have rendered this entire process of sharing my memories impossible, as I could have never laid out the details in any but the most generic of ways. The fact that I have to this day most everything I've ever written and collected is a true miracle in and of itself, especially considering the very high number of household moves I've made in my life prior to joining the Air Force, as well as during my twenty year military career and the past seventeen years since my retirement.

My best advice to anyone who thinks theirs is a unique experience worth writing about someday is to get the details down in digital form somewhere online for safekeeping in case your hardcopy memories are ever lost. That way, you'll always have a saved time capsule of memories of your many adventures in life.

~~~~~~~~~~

Jim's House, Queen Anne Hill, Seattle, WA

~~~~~~~~~~

Wednesday, May 23, 1979

1,000 dollars available for my adventure

36 dollars spent this day, 964 dollars remaining

~~~~~~~~~~

The quote of the day comes from my most recent Chinese fortune cookie from dinner with Bruce last week:

~~~~~~~~~~

"Success depends upon hard work"

~~~~~~~~~~

Here are all the other fortune cookie quotes I've collected over the past year:

~~~~~~~~~~

"Do not overtax your powers"

"You will not be lucky for a while"

"Your determination will make you succeed in everything"

"Your efforts will result in much profit"

"Long life and success"

"You are a real leader rather than a follower"

"Your personal finances will be greatly improved"

"A journey by land"

~~~~~~~~~~

I've started collecting addresses of people who have helped me prepare for this new adventure so far:

~~~~~~~~~~

Verla Houston, President of Sundial Travel of Seattle, Inc., 6601 Roosevelt Way NE, Seattle, WA 98115

Bob Rogen, Early Winters, 300 Queen Anne Ave N, Seattle WA 98103

~~~~~~~~~~

I spent $36.00 today at the grocery store for medicines and toiletries for the trip so I'll be prepared out on the road. You just can't leave without having the right stuff for the trip. Now I'm debating if I should just tour Southern England and then make a mad dash to the Continent - perhaps going to Paris and then maybe down to Switzerland. If I try to go to Scotland, I probably won't have either the time or money to do justice to the Continent. Also, the Mediterranean area sounds better every day.

I'm in much better spirits now that I'm away from work. I also bought a Swiss Army Knife today, packed up all my things and made an inventory of what I'm bringing on the trip that I'll enter later. My legs hurt from jogging, but they have not given me any problems on my long walks lately. My knees were pounded too much from the jogging I think, but at least my shin splints are gone.

The main problem remaining is my left thigh above my knee and I think that I must have strained or bruised the muscle - but with luck it should be okay as my legs are very strong these days regardless of these recent troubles. My lower back is also sore and I think it comes from walking up all these hills. It has always been the weakest part of my body, and I should be doing more sit-ups and reverse stretches.

I put the second coat of seam sealant on the tent today and will pack it up in the morning. It looks to be an excellent tent. I'm bringing a lot of clothes with me, including four dress shirts. One must never travel without being able to look good when invited to dinners, etc. Impressions are of great importance and besides, think about all those young, beautiful European women just waiting for me over there - yeah, right! A poor attempt at a joke. I will have to spend the next few days writing letters to people so they know that I'm leaving for Europe. Only six days now...

~~~~~~~~~~

2018 Editorial Comment: While I'm not into fortune cookie sayings per se, I did collect these notes from dinner with my Seattle friend Bruce, as they were for the most part positive and inspiring. Such notes could apply to anyone's life, but I saved them because they reinforced my normally positive and optimistic way of looking at life. After all, how we see the world around us is a choice and I like to use the *anything's possible* frame of mind more often than not.

It was also important to me early on to credit the people who were helping me with my adventure, as I purchased my ticket overseas on Pan Am from Verla Houston at Sundial Travel of Seattle, Inc., and purchased most of my gear at Early Winters outfitters from Bob Rogen. I had a feeling that much of the success of my adventure overseas would depend on the assistance of others, just as *The Great Adventure* had been in 1976-1977. I was beginning to make the connection that my experiences in life were less about me and more about those who had helped or were helping me out along the way.

During the time I was purchasing gear and getting my bike ready for the trip, I didn't really spend much time riding it for conditioning. My habit at the time was to walk down from Queen Anne Hill into downtown Seattle, and figured all the walking and jogging I was doing would essentially provide me with all the conditioning I'd need. While this was true to a certain extent, my body would feel like a truck hit me after the first handful of real days on the road heading to Oxford and down to Christchurch on the South Coast, so perhaps I should have ridden more in preparation.

My comments about dress shirts and European women were wishful thinking, as everything seemed to be so exotic overseas and my comment was more whimsy and dreams than anything of substance - especially on this adventure. However, years later, I'd meet my future wife on the very first day of my first overseas assignment in the United States Air Force to West Germany in

August 1983, so perhaps I'd only crossed wires with a future unknown adventure to me in another time and place...

I'd later make the connection back to many of my previous experiences, and wonder how the similarities and coincidences of one event seemed to dovetail into yet another completely unrelated future episode of my life, pondering if these glimpses had somehow been sneak previews of future attractions. While I'll never know for sure in the here and now what the answer is, I do know there seems to have always been a larger plan my life was fitting into. In that light, I'm confident I've been allowed these glimpses into my future at times as a way to always keep me moving forward in my life, just as I'd always wanted to take this follow-on bicycle adventure overseas to the U.K. and the Continent. In like manner, my friend Laura told me something back at Michigan State University during Winter Term 1976 that I've never forgotten: *"Maybe you should write another poem. I hope you're saving all of them. Maybe someday you could write a book..."*

~~~~~~~~~~

Jim's House, Queen Anne Hill, Seattle, WA

~~~~~~~~~~

Sunday, May 27, 1979

Total: 36 dollars

~~~~~~~~~~

Only two days left. I've missed a few days here in this log and in the meantime I played some tennis with Josh, walked around Greenlake and have been working on an excellent tan. I drew a picture of a wizard that turned out very well. Here's my European Bicycle Trip Inventory:

~~~~~~~~~~

Wear on the flight:

One pair Levi's

One blue & white striped dress shirt

One pair Nike shoes

One pair socks

One pair underwear

One belt

One comb

One pair Ray-Ban prescription glasses

Two gold chains (could help pay for my ticket home...)

One wallet with dollars, traveler's checks, credit cards and my driver's license (I had wanted to buy pound notes prior to leaving, but don't recall I actually did.)

One passport

~~~~~~~~~~

General:

One bicycle (boxed)

Two bike racks

Two Eclipse mounting brackets

One air pump

Three water bottles

One extra wire cable

One front Eclipse bag and mounting hardware rack

One Swiss Army Knife

One logbook

One diary

One 35mm Konica camera

Four rolls of color film

Two rolls of black and white film

One English-French dictionary

One pair of Ray-Ban prescription sunglasses

One spare pair of Ray-Ban prescription clear glasses

One flashlight

One spare bulb

Two spare batteries

Four pens

One hairbrush

Four maps

One address book

One sleeping bag

One sleeping pad

One nylon draw-string bag

One combination lock

One bicycle cable

~~~~~~~~~~~~

Front Eclipse Pannier #1:

One long sleeve wool shirt

One long sleeve flannel shirt

One long sleeve Levi's shirt

Three long sleeve dress shirts (blue/green/brown & white stripes)

~~~~~~~~~~~~

Front Eclipse Pannier #2:

One Gore-Tex rain jacket

One pair cotton shorts

Two nylon running shorts

One swim suit

Six pair underwear

Four pair socks

~~~~~~~~~~~~

Rear Eclipse Pannier #1:

One shaving cream

One razor

Nine spare razor blades

One toothbrush

One toothpaste

One large bar of soap

One deodorant

One shampoo

One rinse

One conditioner

One wash cloth

One spare inner tube

One eight inch crescent wrench

One 7mm Allen wrench

One pedal wrench

One screw driver

One pair of pliers

Four double ended wrenches

Four tent stakes

One Swiss Army knife

One fork

One spoon

One knife

One can opener

One JanSport t-shirt

One Adidas t-shirt

One Property of MSU t-shirt

One Michigan t-shirt

One Seattle Sounders t-shirt

One Rugby shirt

One MSU cutoff football jersey

Two MSU cutoff mesh football jerseys

One Property of MSU shirt

One Michigan cutoff mesh jersey

One red mesh tank top

One pair tennis shoes

One down vest

~~~~~~~~~~

Rear Eclipse Pannier #2:

Three pair Levi's

One pair Levi's cutoffs

One windbreaker

One wind pants

One Cagoule rain poncho

Two rain gaiters

One wool hat

Two rain covers

One towel

One belt

One Frisbee

One spare inner tube

One tire patch kit

One roll of toilet paper

~~~~~~~~~~

Medicine Kit:

1 roll gauze bandage

1 roll adhesive tape

6 gauze bandage pads

5 insect repellent towelettes

3 small bars of soap

2 antibiotic ointment packs

6 salt tablet packs

6 Bayer Aspirin packs

1 razor blade

1 flashlight bulb

2 fingernail clippers

2 fingernail files

1 Blistex lip balm

1 tweezer

1 box Ex-Lax

3 rolls of Rolaids

1 bottle of Bayer Aspirin

10 Contac cold capsules

1 bottle of antiseptic

1 bottle of multi-vitamins

1 bottle of nose spray

1 bottle of eye drops

1 box of Band-Aids

1 box of Sucrets lozenges

1 pair of scissors

1 first aid manual

~~~~~~~~~~~

2018 Editorial Comment: I knew I was bringing a lot of gear with me, but had no idea how long or what the conditions would be during my adventure, as there was no way of predicting either outcome. I had to be prepared to camp out and for all weather conditions, but beyond that, there was no way of knowing what I'd find overseas. In theory, I could have extended my trip out for as long as possible if there had been a way, or everything could have fallen apart in a week - it was all a guess as to how it would go.

I felt like I was ready now for most anything, yet I was already spending the money I'd saved for my trip. Granted, acquiring supplies counted towards trip preparations, but I'd always paid for those types of expenses out of the money I had in my checking account - now I was down to only the money I was bringing with me on the trip. The previous few weeks since leaving Electricraft Stereo had gone through my cash reserves while getting ready for the trip and paying off final bills, so there was some trepidation there as to how much money I had left for the trip itself. That was my reality at the time and I'd just have to deal with the outcome however I could.

~~~~~~~~~~

Chapter Two - Jim's House, Queen Anne Hill, Seattle, WA, to London Heathrow, and Farnham Common, Buckinghamshire, England, U.K.

~~~~~~~~~~

Tuesday, May 29, 1979 and Wednesday, May 30, 1979

Days 1 & 2

Prior to Departing

207 dollars, Total: 243 dollars = 121 pounds, 50 pence

~~~~~~~~~~

15 Miles

26 pence, Total: 121 pounds, 76 pence

~~~~~~~~~~

On the road again! This morning I woke up at 7:00 a.m. Seattle time, with a mild hangover from the red wine and celebrations of the night before with Jim at Venetti's Italian Restaurant & Pizzeria. Ned was going to take me to the airport, but John called and offered me a ride instead. I ate a hot dog, walked to Early Winters to buy some straps for the tent, and then walked over to the Seattle Center and watched the Sonics practice in the Coliseum. They looked good. (The Captain on the plane later said they won by 2 points in overtime and now hold a 3-1 series lead.) Then I ate some ice cream at the Food Circus in the Seattle Center and walked back up Queen Anne Hill to Jim's house.

John picked me up at 3:00 p.m. and took me to the airport. The Pan Am 747 departed Seattle-Tacoma International Airport (Sea-Tac) at 7:00 p.m. I had a window seat and sat beside a couple from Eugene, Oregon, who were planning to drive around England. The flight was very smooth and the route was called the Polar Route over Canada and Greenland. A one-way ticket cost me $207.00 with an open return for my return flight to Seattle. We had two meals during the flight - chicken with rice for dinner during the flight, along with a Continental breakfast shortly before landing. I had maybe three hours of sleep, if that, on the plane during the flight over. We arrived at London Heathrow at 12:00 noon, which was 4:00 a.m. Seattle time.

I picked up my luggage - the box with my disassembled bicycle and bike bags - and went over to a corner of Heathrow's International Arrivals Terminal where I was out of everyone's way and put my bike together, which took a good hour all together. I met an Australian guy who had just bicycled through England and was going home: Gavin, Surrey Rd, Wilson, Perth, West Australia. Then I spent 26 pence on a phone call to my mom's pen pal's house to tell them I arrived safely at Heathrow.

After my bike was put together and I was finally ready to go, I walked the bike out of the airport and rode through the tunnel that runs under the A4 just north of Heathrow. The brakes on the bike are still in bad shape, as they keep pulling to one side. The 50 pound load on the bike is a heavy load, but it's well distributed and the overall center of gravity of the bike is low which helps with stability

The sleeping bag and pad are in the nylon draw-string bag versus the backpack on our previous trip around the U.S., which looks better and cuts down on wind drag. One tire was flat out of the box when I put the bike together in the terminal, but I kept pumping it up every three miles or so since it was a slow leak and I didn't want to start out the trip by having to first change a flat tire.

It had been raining while I was in the airport, but the weather was only overcast and quite humid with a temperature probably in the low 60's when I left the airport. I rode west through Slough in medium to heavy traffic, and soon mastered the left side of the road and the traffic circles. Then I rode north on the A355 for a bit - I don't have a map with me showing any of these roads - until the weather looked like it would pour down rain any minute.

I was in a beautiful area of old, private homes, all hidden by dense hedges with their own private lanes. I went up to one of the houses and asked for water and information on camping possibilities in the area. The lady of the house, Bet, offered to let me camp on their wooded property behind the house and took me around back to show it to me after first putting on her Wellingtons.

As we were looking at the patch of woods it started to rain and having given up on that project she invited me in for a cup of coffee. Her nephew David and his girlfriend Jayne were there, and Bet's brother George stopped by as well. We all talked around the kitchen table, and drank gin and tonics and ate some snacks while watching the rain. Bet decided it would be best if I just stayed in one of their guest rooms for the night and proceeded to prepare dinner.

Her husband, Ian, came home a little bit later and we had a few more drinks before dinner. Dinner was roast lamb which was rolled and stuffed, fresh peas and carrots, potatoes, and for pudding (dessert) a combination of everything available: sliced bananas with real cream, ice cream, mince torte or something like that, and a small slice of pie - an excellent dinner which was followed by after-dinner drinks, liqueurs, fine chocolates and mints.

Following dinner, we watched some telly (television) in the lounge with a roaring fire going in the fireplace. The European Soccer Cup Finals were on and Nottingham Forest won the match. It was decided I would go into London tomorrow with David, Jayne and Ian - as Ian was driving into the City to work the next morning.

After a while the jet lag caught up with me, and Bet brought me upstairs and showed me to a recently renovated and beautiful guest bedroom. It was a very large house that was originally built in 1934 - with gardens, a swimming pool and woods surrounding the back of the property. Bet apologized and said the upstairs was a mess because they were in the process of installing central heating, but the house looked in excellent condition to me.

I settled into my room for a much needed sleep in a beautifully and tastefully decorated guest bedroom - with coordinating duvet cover, curtains and wallpaper - just as the sun set through leaded glass windows overlooking the gardens behind the house. Tomorrow we're off to London for sightseeing to see the sights on foot and by double-decker bus.

My quote of the day, *"Everything is the same and everything is different."* What a wonderful introduction to England!

~~~~~~~~~~

<u>2018 Editorial Comment</u>: I have many observations from the start of my overseas bicycle adventure in 1979 and of this day in particular, but first I'll begin with a few basic housekeeping items for my account of this trip and then discuss my thoughts about this day in particular.

My daily logbook entries for this trip were quite detailed in the beginning and tapered off as the trip progressed, as you'll soon discover that many of my days on the road were quite taxing with difficult conditions at the time. I've edited these daily accounts for readability and story structure in order to expand what often were abbreviated notes and entries at the time, while at the same time filling in the gaps. I still remember many of the details about each day as if they took place only a short time ago. Adventures have a way of locking in certain memories that stand out as unique experiences forever in one's mind, while other routine and non-important events fade into background memories without anything particular to note about them.

I personally love to use the individual country names of my experiences in the United Kingdom - *England, Scotland and Wales* - as they have such a romantic and historical ring to them in my mind the generic abbreviation U.K. can't touch or come close to. Each region has such a unique personality and even landscape representing its geography, people, population centers, infrastructure, and history that the individual country names capture so well.

Many of my reflections back in the day of my adventure through the U.K. and France need to be seen within the timeframe I was experiencing them in 1979 and within the light of how things were back in the day - especially how they appeared to me at the time on my first trip overseas. I've returned to the U.K. many times since my initial bicycle adventure and our family lived in England for almost eight years while I was stationed there in the United States Air Force, so I've experienced much of the change that's taken place since my initial adventure in 1979.

With each day's Editorial Comment I'll attempt to set the stage as to my personal experiences and impressions, and how they captured a snapshot in time during my visit, as well as, how things have moved on since then. The year 1979 was not so far removed from the heyday of the 1960s, nor was it in many cases that far removed from the postwar period of the 1950s, as it seemed like time stood still in many of the rural villages and throughout the countryside.

I remember wondering how this trip was going to work out as I claimed my bike box from the baggage claim area and made my way over to a corner of the International Arrivals Terminal to put it together. I found an area in the hall there by the windows where there was less foot traffic so I wouldn't be in anyone's way, and began pulling out all the bike parts and pieces from the large box there onto the polished tile floor to gather together my bike parts, tools, paniers and bags prior to assembling them.

This process took a good hour as I watched the rain and dreary overcast skies through the large picture windows of the hall, wondering how this was all going to work out. Gavin came over to me and told me about his bicycle trip that he'd just completed, which gave me encouragement, but at the same time, I wondered where I'd sleep and camp here in the greater London area, as I didn't have a clue at the time.

The map I had to use was a large scale map of the British Isles, with inserts of some of the larger cities and streets, so most of the lesser roads in the London area weren't depicted on it. My initial plan was to ride northwest from London Heathrow to the town of Berkhamsted where my mom's pen pal lived in Hertfordshire. They'd been pen pals for decades and my plan was to go see them and somehow find my bearings to determine a plan for my adventure.

While I wanted to see all of the British Isles on this trip, I also knew I had less money with me than I'd hoped to have for the journey, so I'd vacillated back and forth between focusing on the British Isles and the Continent. I wanted to see both and knew I wouldn't be able to with the little money I had, so I wasn't sure where I'd go on this trip. I didn't know any other languages, so I had some trepidation about crossing the English Channel - besides the expense of the ferries - and didn't want to get stranded far away from London Heathrow where I needed to fly out of for my return flight.

I really didn't know very much about my open return Pan Am flight back the States, besides needing enough money to pay for the ticket based on the current exchange rate at the time and scheduling it, so I had to keep enough money in reserve to pay for my way back home. The bottom line was I didn't really know what I was going to do on this trip and didn't have much money either, so everything was up in the air by the time I'd put my bike together and pushed it out of the terminal.

The gist of it all, was that I was setting out on an adventure like I'd never had before and there was no way of knowing how any of it was going to work out, or not. For all I knew, the entire journey would fall apart the minute I rode out of Heathrow, as I really didn't know what to expect. I could see the downsides and possibilities for failure in my mind's eye easily enough, but couldn't even fathom what might qualify as a success.

I wasn't pleased with the fact I had a flat tire right out of the box while putting my bike together, but at the same time, I wasn't willing to take the time to swap out or patch the tube there in the airport. My plan was to keep adding air to the tire every couple of miles and then deal with it later on when I had some time. I pushed my bike through the doors of the terminal into a cool, overcast and humid day, much relieved that it wasn't raining at the time, although the pavement was still wet.

My initial choice of road to ride was pretty much my only choice at the time to go west towards Slough on the *London to Bath Road,* and it didn't take long to figure out how riding on the left side of the road and the roundabouts all worked. From Slough it would be due north to Berkhamsted and the A355 seemed to do the trick. Other than that, there was no rhyme or reason as to the direction I was riding, as it certainly hadn't been planned out in advance - I was just winging it right from the start. From Slough I rode north to Farnham Royal, The Broadway and then to Farnham Common, although I knew nothing about them at the time. (I referenced Google Maps Satellite View online to reconstruct the original route of the trip I'd detailed in my logbook, in order to reference individual town names, landmarks and distances.)

At this point I was feeling pretty tired from being up since the morning of the day before in Seattle and as it was looking like it would pour down rain at any minute, I decided to try and find a place to camp. The area I was in was quite established with very tall hedges and greenery everywhere, such that the houses themselves were all quite private from the road. My approach was to always ask for water at someone's house prior to asking and getting permission to camp somewhere, and at the time it looked like the nearby patch of woods would be my only option for camping in this area - at least it was outside the urban area of London proper.

So I picked the closest house to where I'd stopped and walked up the driveway (it could have been a pea gravel drive, I don't recall) to a very proper two-story home built of brick and timbers that was quite nice but didn't stand out as anything over the top at the time, as it was just properly understated as a very nice home. Bet, the lady of the house, came to the door after I'd knocked and I asked if I could have some water for my water bottle and if I could camp in the woods behind their house. She didn't hesitate for a moment and went to put on her Wellies to go take a look at the wood with me.

We walked together as I pushed my bike back to the rear of her property where the woods began and she was in the process of explaining that I could camp in the general area when it began raining. She immediately said she had a better idea and invited me in to have some coffee instead, which led to the most amazing day for me. It felt like I'd landed in a fairy tale at Bet's house where I was a long-lost and very welcomed guest there for a visit - and from then on everything kept getting better and better until I thought I was dreaming!

David and Jayne were there at the kitchen table and later George stopped by to join us for coffee and snacks, while enjoying quite an animated conversation about my trip, America and life in England - especially when we switched from coffee to gin and tonics while watching it rain. Bet decided that camping was out of the question and said I'd stay in her guest room, and then proceeded to make dinner for everyone there in the kitchen. A plan was made for David and Jayne to show me London the next day, and then Ian came home from work where he was a solicitor or lawyer in London, and the evening just flowed into probably the most wonderful meal of my life. I'd never had so many servings, desserts and after dinner drinks, liqueurs, fine chocolates and mints in my life - and of course, I had to sample a little of everything!

The experience was totally like being in an amazing movie and I was simply part of the assembled cast it seemed, as if I belonged there. I observed a few differences at dinner such as the family dining Continental Style and that water wasn't served with the meal, but everything else about England was just about the same as I'd known it growing up except for the accents and a few word differences and pronunciations. It was after dinner when we retired to the lounge that I could tell notable differences while first watching the news and then Nottingham Forest win the European Soccer Cup Finals on the telly. British TV at the time had a totally different feel to it than the American version did, and the accents and commentary told me clearer than anything else that I was in England, as it was all very fascinating to me that I was actually there.

Between the conversation, soccer match and the extremely long day I'd had, I began fading and Bet showed me to my room. She apologized for what she said was a mess during the process of adding central heating, but everything was perfectly in place, and the guest bedroom had been redecorated and beautifully furnished. After showing me where everything was and once I had everything I needed for the night from my bike bags, I settled down to the most wonderful night's sleep.

The leaded glass windows were open a couple of inches letting in the cool evening air, the room was decorated like a palace, the duvet cover was warm and cozy, and this was the start of my overseas bicycle adventure - what an amazing day! While the hospitality and generosity of the British people towards me would continue on in an amazing way during the course of my journey, the physical aspects of my trip would become much more difficult as the days wore on - as this would be the wettest spring and early summer people could remember - but as for this day, I was on top of the world!

~~~~~~~~~~

A Day of Sightseeing in London

~~~~~~~~~~~

Thursday, May 31, 1979   Day 3

60 Miles, Total: 75 Miles

3 pounds, 10 pence, Total: 124 pounds, 86 pence

~~~~~~~~~~~

Last night when I finally crawled into bed under the lofty down of the duvet, I discovered that Bet had already warmed it earlier with an electric blanket for me. The leaded glass windows were cracked open a little, which soon cooled the room in the evening air and I immediately drifted off to sleep. Bet's soft knock at the door at 7:00 a.m. the next morning woke me up and she handed me a cup of freshly brewed coffee in bed, and said breakfast would be ready in a few minutes. I had been dozing in and out of sleep since 4:30 a.m. from the singing of the birds and the sunrise streaming in through the open, leaded glass windows, and had never before experienced the luxury of waking up to a fresh cup of coffee in bed - what a beautiful morning!

I quickly bathed and put on a fresh shirt, and then went downstairs to enjoy a breakfast of Rice Krispies with tea and toast, along with David, Jayne and Bet. Ian came down for breakfast shortly afterwards and then David, Jayne and I all drove into London with Ian in his beautiful Jaguar sedan with leather seats. It was an hour drive from Farnham Common into the City through rush hour traffic and Ian dropped the three of us off at Westminster Abbey for a day of sightseeing. Ian was a solicitor, or

57

lawyer, in the City and today was a normal workday for him. My initial impression of London was it was very old and filled with narrow streets, crazy drivers and air pollution. The historic stone buildings are currently in the process of being cleaned of the black, sooty film that covers many of them, revealing pristine stonework underneath once the soot has been removed. I was soon caught up in the intoxicating pulse of City life as we began our sightseeing tour on foot, and I quickly became mesmerized at the sights, sounds and atmosphere of one of the world's greatest cities.

We toured Westminster Abbey, saw Big Ben and the Palace of Westminster, and paid a visit to Number 10 Downing Street - only from the street outside the official residence - but were unable to see Prime Minister Margaret Thatcher while we were there. Then it was off to see the Changing of the Horse Guards, St. James Park, St. James Palace, Buckingham Palace, Nelson's Column in Trafalgar Square, Piccadilly Circus, Leicester Square and the West End, and then had fish and chips for lunch for 1 pound, 80 pence. After lunch we saw St. Paul's Cathedral and spent 30 pence to see the Catacombs, and then saw the Monument to the Great Fire of London or the Monument, the Fish Market, the Tower of London, the Tower Bridge, and an old marina followed by a boat tour on the River Thames for 75 pence. Our river tour ended at Westminster Abbey after an informative description of all the buildings along the banks of the Thames - after which I tipped the Captain 25 pence (an estimate, as I hadn't recorded the amount) for his exceptional narrative.

We spent the entire day from 9:30 a.m. until 6:30 p.m. walking the streets of London - except for lunch and the 20 minute boat tour. Ian picked us up again at our arranged meeting spot and it was back to the house for gin and tonics prior to a dinner of roast beef, cabbage, potatoes, gravy and red wine, along with a pudding of marmalade cakes covered in liqueur, followed by more after dinner liqueurs. David and Jayne retired upstairs, Ian fell asleep watching the news on the telly, and Bet and I stayed up for a while talking before I decided it was time for me to go to sleep after another wonderful day in England!

(Bet, Ian and her brother George, Collinswood Road, Farnham Common, Bucks)

(David, Mudeford Lane, Christchurch, Dorset)

(Jayne, Marmion Green, Somerford, Christchurch, Dorset)

~~~~~~~~~~

2014 Editorial Comment: Most of the photos I took on this bicycle adventure were ruined while going through the X-Ray machines in customs on my return, as I was unaware that I could hand-carry film canisters to avoid potentially exposing the film and ruining it going through customs - live and learn. The two best photos I took during the trip that survived, will be used on the covers of these two volumes of my bicycle adventure to England, Scotland, Wales and France, as I'm quite fond of them.

~~~~~~~~~~

2018 Editorial Comment: While I would like to fully acknowledge everyone 39 years ago for their hospitality in taking such good care of me on my bicycle adventure with their full name and address, I realize in this day of age I need to abbreviate the details of the people I met who helped me out during my journey. One day, if they or their children ever read this book, they'll at least know I remembered them and have always appreciated their gracious support during my travels and will always appreciate it!

I wish I could have kept in contact with everyone over the years, but it was difficult enough just keeping up with my own life during the following years. In the days, weeks, months and years after this adventure, I was either on the road on follow-on adventures, studying to get my degree in school as a poor college student or pursuing a challenging career of flying jets as a navigator in the United States Air Force. My thanks and gratitude, however, go out to everyone for such wonderful memories of your gracious hospitality during my first overseas trip!

This was the most amazing day, starting with my being woken up and given a cup of coffee in bed - what a civilized custom! That morning dozing in and out of sleep as the sun came up, with bird song in the garden just outside the slightly opened leaded glass windows was as nice a morning as I've ever had. I thought I was in a waking dream it was so nice. After breakfast the drive into London in the backseat of Ian's Jaguar was very luxurious, even if the traffic was crazy on the commute into the City.

My initial few minutes of impressions after being dropped off in downtown London with David and Jayne just outside Westminster Abbey in 1979 was one of disappointment, as the traffic was bumper to bumper, the air pollution was overwhelming, all the buildings were covered in filthy black soot and it felt like the place was really run down. It only took a few minutes to step away from the road to gain a new perspective though, as once we reached a quieter and calmer place I began to take it all in and gained a fond appreciation for what was one of the world's greatest cities.

The black soot was being cleaned from the buildings one stone block at a time, revealing the most beautiful pristine stone underneath. It was obvious that if the City kept up with the cleaning, it would completely transform and beautify the City. Once the rush hour snarl of traffic subsided, the streets regained some of their charm and the air pollution seemed to subside a bit as well. As we began our walking tour of all the famous sights, sounds and wonderful tastes and flavors of what was London, it was clear that the City was like a history museum of nonstop cultural sites and I loved it!

We ended up walking all day long, except for a city tour on a double-decker bus, and I enjoyed everything I saw, especially the boat ride as the Captain was such an entertaining and knowledgeable chap. His narrative of everything we were seeing along the River Thames was well worth listening to, as he was a wealth of historical information about the waterfront and surrounding portions of London. We stopped at a traditional English pub for lunch and I loved the delicious fish and chips I had. By the time Ian picked us up in the late afternoon we were plenty tired and ready for the drive home.

The day just continued getting better when it didn't even seem possible, as Bet served up another wonderful dinner and after the news on the telly, Bet and I talked for quite a while before I called it a night. It would be a regular occurrence for me to stay up late into the evening discussing everything under the sun with the folks who'd taken me in during my journey and one I very much enjoyed. I really didn't know what to make of my wonderful arrival experience during the first two days I was in England, but I knew it was very special indeed and really endeared the British Isles and its people to me in a way that would last a lifetime!

~~~~~~~~~~~

Chapter Three - Farnham Common, Buckinghamshire, to Berkhamsted, Hertfordshire

~~~~~~~~~~

Friday, June 1, 1979   Day 4

25 Miles, Total: 100 Miles

0 pounds, 0 pence, Total: 124 pounds, 86 pence

~~~~~~~~~~

Needless to say, I slept very well last night, and got up around 8:00 a.m. when Bet woke me up and brought me a cup of coffee in bed again this morning. After showering, I had Frosted Flakes, toast and tea for breakfast, and then said goodbye to David, Jayne and Ian as they were all leaving soon afterwards. I changed my front tire, only to find that the new one was also flat. So I changed the inner tube again and patched the two bad ones as well. Then I said thank you and goodbye to Bet, and rode down the lane and north on the A355 in the direction of Chesham and then on to Berkhamsted.

When I arrived in Berkhamsted I couldn't find Shootersway or Barncroft Road, as I was using a detailed map of the entire British Isles that only showed the major highways and towns. I stopped to ask an elderly man on a park bench for directions and he said that he was not only from out of town, but that he was blind as well. I thanked him for the conversation and went on to ask another man who pointed me in the right direction. I was pushing my bike up a steep hill when a white Jaguar passed by and stopped, backed up and out stepped Marny, my mom's pen pal. Her daughter Jackie was with her in the car and they showed me the way to their house in the car as I followed behind them on my bike for about two or three blocks.

I helped unload their groceries into the house and then we all went shopping in Chester. Later after returning home, Lloyd came home and we had sweet and sour chicken, chips, peas, milk, and lemon meringue pie along with a different meringue, fruit and cream dessert. Then Lloyd and I took Jackie to the train station to visit a friend for the evening, while Lloyd and I went to meet Mark at the local tavern. At the pub I was introduced to Tim and Andy, and later we went to Tim's flat to listen to a radio broadcast of the *The Never Never Band* that Andy used to belong to. Andy is now a solo artist and keyboard player, and he invited me to attend his recording sessions on Tuesday and Wednesday.

Afterwards we went to another pub, before meeting Jackie and returning home. After relaxing and enjoying some coffee with a few cakes and sweets back home, Marny came home and we had some more coffee before retiring to bed for the evening where I'm now writing the account of today's trip in bed. That's all for tonight.

~~~~~~~~~~

2018 Editorial Comment: This was another amazing day, as I still remember Marny and Jackie passing by me in their white Jaguar while I was pushing my bike up a steep rise in the road into Berkhamsted. Marny slowed the car and then stopped as I caught up to them, and then I rode after them all the way to their house. My mom and Marny had been pen pals for decades, and there was so much to talk about over coffee, sweets and more sweets!

The entire family was very welcoming and the night out at the pub with Lloyd and Mark was really fun, as it was their treat to introduce me to pub life for the first time, even though I didn't drink much. This tavern wasn't a sedate restaurant type environment but rather a bar and draft beer type of atmosphere, with peanut shells all over the floor, loud music, pinball type machines and round tables for small gatherings - even then it was so loud you could hardly carry on a conversation.

Meeting Tim and Andy was an inspirational moment for me, as Andy invited me to attend his recording sessions as a solo artist, and remains active in the music business today. As a result of meeting Andy and attending his recording sessions, the logbook of my overseas trip is filled up with more original song lyrics and verses I'd written during my journey than actual logbook entries. These verses I'd scribbled out during my trip eventually made it into my *Book Two - The Early Years (My Early Lyrics and Poems)*.

This adventure turned out to be a very inspirational time for me with a tremendous burst of creative energy and vivid dreams on this trip. I also drew lots of graphic art type doodles and little drawings in my logbook during the trip, and so far I've used one of them as the design basis for one of the paintings I painted back in 2015.

~~~~~~~~~~

Berkhamsted, Hertfordshire

~~~~~~~~~~

Saturday, June 2, 1979   Day 5

0 Miles, Total: 100 Miles

0 pounds, 0 pence, Total: 124 pounds, 86 pence

~~~~~~~~~~

Here's what happened today. I got up and had breakfast, where I met Marny's husband, Jim - and afterwards Jim and Jackie went to the store. Marny did her ironing while I mowed and raked the lawn. Then Jackie and I spent some time sunbathing on lounge chairs in the middle of the back yard during the early afternoon while listening to the radio and among other shows, the *American Top 40*. It's Jackie's 18th birthday tomorrow and she's a very pretty girl who's planning to go to college to become a store window dresser/designer. Her brother Lloyd is a car salesman, while her other brother Mark is looking into becoming a cigarette representative.

After sunbathing, I went for a walk down the road and enjoyed looking out over the classic English countryside surrounding Berkhamsted. Later Marny, Jim and I had a dinner of fish, potatoes, beets and salad - along with three desserts. It was very good and although I've never acquired a taste for beets, I have become quite fond of the fish I've had here in England. Jackie was out with her boyfriend tonight and Lloyd was out for the evening as well. After dinner Marny's father came over to the house, and later on Marny's cousin Frances and her husband John stopped by and gave me some advice on everything that I should see on my tour of Southern England. Here's the list he wrote down and explained to me:

~~~~~~~~~

John's Travel Log of Southern England's Highlights to See

- Oxford

- Stratford-upon-Avon

- Cheltenham

- Bath

- Wells

- Somerset

- Devon

- Cornwall

- Exeter

- Dorset

- Dorchester

- Poole

- New Forest

- Salisbury

- Winchester

- Mid-Sussex

- Canterbury

- Kent down to Dover

~~~~~~~~~~

Just a short sightseeing list for me. In the end, I did see a number of these areas and towns during my journey, and even more during my later visits and while living in the U.K.

Then I watched some telly and enjoyed a program on English athletics, followed by a Rod Stewart special. Marny and I then had tea and talked for a while, and soon afterwards I went to bed. Here are a few observations that I've noticed so far about life in England:

- The English dine Continental Style using the knife and fork at the same time, as opposed to the American version of using the knife and fork for cutting food and then switching to using the fork alone to eat it with.

- There are public footpaths throughout the English countryside for walking through the fields, as well as bridle paths for horseback riding through the countryside.

- The English know much more about America than we know about England.

- English accents and mannerisms are much more pronounced than our American versions are.

- British telly only has three channels - two run by the BBC and one independent station that shows a few commercials like our TV networks do.

- English radio seems to be run mostly by the BBC, but I think there are 'pirate radio stations' located off the coast in the North Sea and/or the English Channel, too.

- Driver's Education Training isn't free here like ours which is conducted in our high schools - in England it costs 4 pounds/hour and is taught by private instructors.

That's all for today.

~~~~~~~~~~

2018 Editorial Comment: I remember it being a really nice day and quite hot, as after breakfast and meeting Jim, I mowed their good sized yard with a manual push mower and then raked it afterwards. After that good workout, it was nice to do some sunbathing with Jackie and share viewpoints about pop music and everything under the sun from both sides of the Atlantic. I also enjoyed my walk to the edge of town to look out across the English Countryside, as it felt magical that I was even there to see it. The evening seemed to be full of nonstop visitors popping by and conversation, which was very nice and John gave me quite a list of recommended sights to see across Southern England.

I began the day's logbook entry with an entire long song lyric that I'd written *"I don't want to leave without you by my side..."* and ended the day's entry with my observations about some of the differences between English and American life. This entire trip was a time of exceptional creative energy for me, at least in my mind and my logbook is full of scraps of lyrics I'd written and graphic design type drawings I wanted to paint one day. One of those drawings actually came to life in 2015 when I painted a cityscape of Seattle that I'm quite proud of.

While the loud pub scene really wasn't my style, I had a good time with Lloyd and Mark, and enjoyed meeting Tim and Andy. I was especially looking forward to attending Andy's recording session on Tuesday, which was no doubt fueling my subconscious to begin writing song lyrics again. My tea with Marny at the end of the day after everyone else had left or gone to bed, was a nice way of finishing the day over conversation and a few biscuits (cookies). An enjoyable way to finish off the day!

~~~~~~~~~~

Berkhamsted, Hertfordshire

~~~~~~~~~~~~

Sunday, June 3, 1979   Day 6

40 Miles | Total: 140 Miles

0 pounds, 0 pence | Total: 124 pounds, 86 pence

~~~~~~~~~~~~

I got up this morning and Marny fixed me a breakfast of sausage, toast and scrambled eggs. I think that I've already had this year's allotment of tea and coffee - roughly every 15 minutes or so - but I could get used to this. Marny, Jim and I drove downtown and watched the filming of a movie (in the town of Chesham I think), and saw the film director, Otto Preminger, from a distance. Then we drove over to the ruins of an old castle and went on a scenic drive through the countryside. At home we had a warm lunch of leg of lamb, carrots, cauliflower, potatoes, gravy and two pieces of pie. As we were finishing lunch, Jackie and her boyfriend Tony came home and had lunch as well.

After lunch we went to a local museum where the highlighted attraction was a pair of dressed fleas. Then we drove around the countryside on a second scenic tour and stopped in at the local sweet shop. Marny enjoys her sweets as she always has pies, cakes, tarts, ice cream, candy, chocolate and everything else at home for everyone to enjoy - quite nice, actually. Once we returned home we had some ice cream. Lloyd and Sally joined us for dinner for a banquet of leftovers, along with many types of desserts.

After dinner we went to the local pub, where we talked with Andy and some other folks. After the pub we watched the telly and Marny brought out a Horoscope book to look through with me. It seems that I'm the sign of a Monkey in China and a Taurus - both seem to have brought me good luck so far, as this trip has been very enjoyable! Here are a few more observations I've made:

- British telly is very conservative and different from ours back home, but they do show American TV shows here as well.

- Americans shower every day but that doesn't seem to be the case here, probably because the water costs more.

- England has many different newspapers, and lots of them seem to be tabloid style papers.

- It's very interesting to view America from a distance and through the eyes and viewpoints of other people and countries. It's refreshing and enlightening to look at your own country from another perspective. I find that I miss hearing the news about the States, and pay close attention to it anytime they mention America on the telly, radio or in the papers.

~~~~~~~~~~

2018 Editorial Comment: I was being exceptionally well taken care of during my stay with Marny and would have set out the next day to resume my bike trip if it hadn't been for Andy's invitation to attend his recording session on the following Tuesday. I was well aware I needed to do something to earn my keep so to speak, and gladly mowed and raked the lawn the previous day. Theirs was a nice suburban style brick home and lawn, and it was the least I could do for everyone being so good to me.

Marny seemed to have made a plan for most of the rest of the days and pulled out all the stops with her meal planning, as they were delicious. It was very interesting to watch Otto Preminger on the film set in town and to take scenic drives through the countryside - and of course the visit to the museum and sweet shop!

As everything in England was new to me, if only in a different style or presentation, I was always comparing and contrasting what I saw and experienced with what I knew back in the States. I quickly picked up being able to understand the variances and nuances between regional differences in the English accent and our American English, but at times I came across someone on this trip that wasn't quite as easy to understand - especially in Scotland and Wales. It was all such an adventure for me and my trip through Day 6 was as enjoyable as most anything I'd ever done before in my life - just a wonderful experience!

~~~~~~~~~~

~~~~~~~~~~

Monday, June 4, 1979   Day 7

20 Miles | Total: 160 Miles

0 pounds, 0 pence | Total: 124 pounds, 86 pence

~~~~~~~~~~

I slept in today until noon, which was very lazy - must still be the jet lag. Then I got up and had coffee and toast, read the paper, and went out and swept Marny's long driveway. Lloyd came home for lunch and Marny made me some scrambled eggs. Afterwards, Lloyd went back to work, and Marny and I drove downtown for some film and went to the local zoo.

The zoo was a local animal park and the ticket I still have today says *The Zoological Society of London, Whipsnade Park.* (The park has greatly expanded since my visit in 1979, according to my online research and was called *Whipsnade Wild Animal Park* back then. Today it's called *ZSL Whipsnade Zoo*.) We walked around the animal park and Marny took a few Polaroid photos of me at the park, and I enjoyed the visit.

Back at the house we had a minute steak, chips and cabbage along with sautéed onions, green peppers and mushrooms. For dessert we had ice cream along with rice pudding and sliced bananas.

After dinner Marny, Jim, Lloyd, Jackie and I all watched the telly and had more sweets, and now it's off to bed. I'll get up early tomorrow to go watch Andy record in the studio. He's a solo artist who sings and plays all the instruments himself - keyboards, synthesizers and drums. Hopefully the two singles he'll record tomorrow will catch on.

I plan to leave Berkhamsted on Thursday and continue on with my bike trip.

~~~~~~~~~~~

2018 Editorial Comment: This was a very enjoyable day and it was nice spending time with Marny going into town and to the animal park. I hoped that doing a few odd jobs around the house like sweeping the driveway would help offset my staying at Marny's, as they were working class folks, but the recording session would be Tuesday and I really wanted to observe it.

So far my bicycle trip was anything but a hardship, but it certainly was an adventure. I couldn't believe I was actually in England and was getting used to all the differences from what I'd known back in the States. I knew the trip wouldn't stay this nice throughout the adventure, but had no way of knowing how difficult it would turn out to be at times. Had I known then, I would have appreciated even more the pleasant times I'd spent in Farnham Common and Berkhamsted, but there was no way of knowing that ahead of time.

While life on the road would turn out to be difficult at times, especially as I ran out of money towards the end, the British people would remain as nice and generous to me as ever during the entire length of my journey. The only significant difference would be in Scotland, where everything was geared towards youth hostels, which I ended up staying in. I much rather enjoyed the experience of staying on farms as I did throughout England and Wales, but the remote countryside of Scotland wasn't really set up in the same way, especially in the Highlands and along the fiords, as the farmers didn't live far away from the village centers. Besides, there weren't many people in the countryside at all in the outlying areas of Scotland, as the terrain was very rugged and windswept.

The biggest difference maker for much of my journey would be the rain, as the rains began as soon as I departed Berkhamsted riding west in the direction of Oxford...

~~~~~~~~~~

~~~~~~~~~~

Tuesday, June 5, 1979   Day 8

40 Miles | Total: 200 Miles

0 pounds, 0 pence | Total: 124 pounds, 86 pence

~~~~~~~~~~

Today I got up around 8:30 a.m., and had a poached egg on toast and coffee for breakfast. Mark came by around 10:00 a.m., and we drove over to Luton, which is about 15 miles NE of Berkhamsted, to watch Andy record his songs. The studio was in an old warehouse and the inside walls had all been soundproofed. Andy worked on two singles: *Nightlife* and *Streetlife.* Dave was the Sound Engineer, and Paul loaned Andy his keyboards to use. Paul was the keyboard player for *The Never Never Band* - formerly called the *Druids* that Andy used to play with. The songs are coming along quite well.

I'm watching everything very carefully and adding all that I see to my list of ideas, as I've always been interested in music - so I'm imagining that I, too, could one day be a musician. Today I had to go downstairs into one of the recording rooms to bring something up for Andy and momentarily pictured myself as an artist recording one day - but then I came back to reality.

Once I returned to Marny's we had chicken, chips, carrots and peas for dinner. Now it's time to write a few letters and watch some telly. There's a good music program on at 10:00 p.m. tonight.

~~~~~~~~~~

2018 Editorial Comment: It was a fascinating experience for me to spend the entire day in the studio with Andy, as it was really a dream come true for me. I'd always been interested in becoming a musician and writing my own songs as a songwriter, and this was my first ever experience in a recording studio. I liked both of the singles Andy was working on that day and studied the recording process of laying down individual tracks, and everything else that studio recording involves.

It would be much later, from 1989-1993, when I would go on to write 250+ or so songs (most are finished, but some have only partial lyric sheets and chords) and then went on to record well over a hundred simple demo tracks while living in the U.K. I always remembered Andy's recording sessions I'd observed in 1979, and while I was quite nervous and unsure of myself during my own recording sessions in the 1990s, I was able to at least capture the essence of the songs I'd written.

There was one more day of recording scheduled in Luton for Andy, so Mark and I made plans to attend that session as well. I made plans to leave Berkhamsted on Thursday to ride towards Oxford, as I had decided to initially focus on Southern England and make a decision later on if I'd go next to the Continent or head up towards Scotland - I figured I wouldn't be able to do both with the little money I had.

While I hadn't spent much money so far on the trip, I knew that wouldn't last long. Based on the cost of everything in England, I understood that once I began spending my traveler's checks each day on the road I'd go through them pretty quickly. Regardless, I would do my best to see everything I could in the time I had remaining, but first there was another recording session of Andy's to attend!

~~~~~~~~~~

Berkhamsted, Hertfordshire

~~~~~~~~~

Wednesday, June 6, 1979   Day 9

40 Miles | Total: 240 Miles

0 pounds, 0 pence | Total: 124 pounds, 86 pence

~~~~~~~~~

I woke up around 10:00 a.m. this morning - another late morning. After a breakfast of toast and coffee, Mark and Cecily stopped by and picked me up. After we dropped off Cecily at her house, Mark and I went over to the studio where Andy, Paul and Dave were already working on Andy's two singles. Dave is the Sound Engineer at Quest Studios, in Luton, England. We spent all day in the studio and had the two songs mixed by 7:00 p.m. Afterwards I decided not to go to the concert by *The Never Never Band* - formerly called the *Druids* which had been Andy's band - and the band that Paul is the keyboard player for now. Andy passed on the concert as well.

Mark and Cecily dropped me off at the house, and Marny prepared chicken and chips for dinner. John and Frances were there as well, and wished me good luck on the rest of my journey. Then we watched some TV and looked at old photo albums of Marny's. Afterwards I started to get my things packed and ready to go in the morning - I hope my luck continues. Here are a few more observations I've had:

- I've noticed that my dreaming at night has been very intense lately and that I can remember many of my dreams once I wake up in the morning.

- I must have gained five pounds so far on this trip, with all of the big dinners and desserts I've had. I'm enjoying it while it lasts, as I'm sure it will be the exception rather than the rule...

(Marny, Jim, Mark & Cecily, Lloyd & Sally, Jackie & Tony, John & Frances and Andy, Berkhamsted, Herts)

Tomorrow my plan is to ride towards Oxford and then decide where to go next from there...

~~~~~~~~~~~

2018 Editorial Comment: The day had really been exceptional having watched the recording process all the way through mixing Andy's two singles *Nightlife* and *Streetlife*. I really enjoyed the opportunity to watch the complete two-day recording process right through mixing the final tracks. The experience only reaffirmed my own desire to one day write music as a songwriter, too.

It was nice to look through old photo albums with Marny and see how life had been for them over the years. She and everyone else had done such a wonderful job of taking care of me at the start of my trip in Berkhamsted, yet I knew it was time to head out and get started on the rest of my adventure. Packing up my bike always felt good, knowing I'd soon be on the road again.

What I couldn't know at the time, was that the relatively pleasant and dry weather conditions I'd experienced so far despite mostly overcast skies wouldn't last long, and I'd be heading out into the wettest late spring and early summer in recent memory...

~~~~~~~~~~

Chapter Four - Berkhamsted, Hertfordshire, to Oxford and Wantage, Oxfordshire

~~~~~~~~~

Thursday, June 7, 1979   Day 10

80 Miles | Total: 320 Miles

0 pounds, 0 pence | Total: 124 pounds, 86 pence

~~~~~~~~~

I got up around 9:00 a.m., washed up and said thank you and goodbye to Jim, and then enjoyed a breakfast of scrambled eggs, toast and coffee. After getting everything together and packing up my bike, I took pictures of Marny and Jackie out in front of the house, and thanked them very much for their hospitality and said goodbye. I then rode down into Berkhamsted under an overcast sky and it started raining as soon as I got out of town. I took the A4251 called the *Aylesbury London Road* and rode on into Aylesbury in the cold rain. Then I took the A418 southwest to Thame, and it continued to sprinkle and rain.

Just outside of Thame (halfway between Aylesbury and Oxford in the area of Albury Tiddington) a huge wall of purple clouds came towards me with thunder and lightning, so I went up to the nearest farmhouse and asked the lady of the house, Ellen, if I could take refuge from the storm. She said yes, and fixed me a cup of coffee and tarts, and I watched the telly with her 5 year old son John while it poured down rain outside. After about 40 minutes it stopped raining, but the clouds were still dark all around us. It was about 3:00 p.m. and I decided to head back out again. I finished my coffee and tarts, said goodbye and thank you to Ellen for having given me refuge from the storm - and rode off down the road.

(Ellen, Albury, Tiddington, Oxford)

I rode down the divided highway called the A40 towards Oxford and it started raining again. The divided highway was very busy with lots of traffic in a rainstorm as I followed it on into Oxford. I was lucky not to have gotten run over while wearing a dark blue raincoat in the very dark afternoon rain. There were lots of trucks going by and I don't think that I was supposed to be on that road. I got into Oxford and it stopped raining for a spell. I saw lots of old, stone buildings and there were students, bicycles and people all around - as well as very busy traffic just like in any other big city.

It started raining again, so I took the first road south out of Oxford called the *Oxford Road* which took me eventually into Abingdon - all in the rain. I ate the apple that Marny had given me before leaving, which was the first food I'd eaten since Ellen's coffee and tarts. Then I took a wrong turn and went down the wrong road - in the rain and clouds I got turned around, and couldn't tell which direction west was - and the map I had was useless on small roads, as it only showed the major highways for all of the British Isles. So instead of going southwest, I started riding east and rode six miles before I figured it out.

I went up to a house for water and directions and met a young German couple with two small children who were very kind to me. She gave me some tea and two pieces of cheesecake and he drew a local map for me. Afterwards I forgot to get their names and address. He worked down the street at the JET Plant - Joint European Tour - as a computer/electronics technician. So with the help of the map he drew for me I rode south to Didcote.

The sun finally came out and there were blue skies in the west. The only other time I've seen the sun here in England was last Saturday at Marny's while sunbathing with Jackie. A rainbow appeared as well, so I knew that all hope had not been lost.

In Didcote I rode west to Wantage, where I turned south for a few miles and stopped at this farm where I'm staying tonight. I went up to the house and met a young couple with a baby, asking her for some water for my water bottles and him for camping directions. He showed me a field on the farm where I could camp, and I asked him if I could sleep in his open barn that had straw spread all around on the ground which was nice and dry. He said ok and so here I am stretched out on the sleeping bag in the straw.

My legs have stiffened up and are very sore, especially my butt, and my neck is also sore, as well as my back, sides, feet and arms. My hand is sore now as well from writing today's journal entry. I also feel like I might be getting pneumonia from being out in the cold rain all day. Isn't this trip just great?! Oh well, what would an adventure be without some hardship? It keeps the riffraff out of the adventure stories. That's all for today - and maybe forever at this rate. I'd better take some aspirin, if I can first get up...

~~~~~~~~~~

2018 Editorial Comment: This turned out to be quite a day, with more packed into it than I would have ever expected as I left

Marny's house to ride west towards Oxford. I'd figured that the southern loop down towards the coast would make a good start, especially as John had given it such glowing reviews in our discussion about where to ride to next.

I hadn't had the opportunity to do any research before my flight to London Heathrow, as to study up on what I wanted to see. The sum total of the British Isles and Europe covered too much territory anyway, especially as I didn't even have an itinerary or the faintest idea where to go. I was just winging it, falling back on my basic understanding of geography and the large scale paper map of the British Isles and parts of France that I had with me, which really didn't give me much of a clue. So in the end, I just followed any road that was going my way...

I figured if I made a pylon turn around Oxford and Bath, then I'd have enough time to figure out if I wanted to make a dash to the Continent or not by the time I reached the south coast. If not, I'd decide where to go next along the coast and/or head north towards Scotland, which was a good distance away. Just letting the trip unfold on its own would hopefully make my decisions easier as to where to go, while at the same time the landscape was beautiful to my eyes everywhere I went.

The dark purple clouds heading from the west towards Albury Tiddington definitely gave me a start, as it looked like something out of tornado alley back in the States. I definitely didn't want to get caught in it and Ellen was a real Godsend as I drank coffee and tarts at her kitchen table as the sky opened up and absolutely poured outside. The weather was not only terrible with the rain and accompanying wind, but the temperature really dropped, as by the time I said thank you and goodbye to Ellen and her son

John after the rain stopped, it was still windy, overcast and quite cold.

I rode on towards Oxford only to feel threatened by the traffic and large trucks in the afternoon darkness wearing a dark blue rain poncho in heavy rain into the center of Oxford. It was nice that I received a reprieve from the rain in Oxford and got a good impression of the bicycles, riders, historic buildings and traffic, but decided this wasn't a place for me to hang around in poor weather and crowded conditions. I made a decision at that point to head south back into the countryside where I hoped to make an easier go of it.

The late afternoon skies were so dark and overcast that I had no idea what the cardinal directions were and got completely turned around heading east when I thought I was riding southwest towards Bath, as my map was of no use to me. The young German couple really saved the day for me, offering me tea and cheesecake and drawing a local map of the area to get me turned back around which I still have today. While the weather had been cold, windy and wet that day, the kindness of complete strangers towards me was really the highlight of the day and my trip.

At the farm where I was offered a field to camp in, I knew I'd much rather just crash on a dry bed of straw with my sleeping bag as I was so tired I didn't want to have to put up the tent. In addition, with the overcast skies and rain that day, I really didn't want to have to deal with the rain if I could get underneath a shelter, which was always my first option and it saved the day for me. This had been my first really tough day on the road and I was dead tired and sore all over.

The weather really took its toll on me as I felt I might be catching pneumonia from exposure in the windy, cold and wet weather. I really needed a good night's sleep and the dry straw was just what I needed. I have a photo of this open shelter on the farm with my bike and sleeping bag spread out on fresh straw under a modern roof structure, which worked out perfectly. Another day on the road, and a healthy dose of reality and life on a bicycle in the middle of an adventure!

~~~~~~~~~~

Chapter Five - Wantage, Oxfordshire, to Marlborough, Wiltshire and Bath, North East Somerset

~~~~~~~~~~

Friday, June 8, 1979   Day 11

80 Miles | Total: 400 Miles

2 pounds, 31 pence | Total: 127 pounds, 17 pence

~~~~~~~~~~

Today was a long day, so here it goes. I went up to the house after getting up at 8:30 a.m., and was offered the opportunity to clean up and have breakfast. I showered and had a nice breakfast of eggs, toast, cereal and coffee. After breakfast, I said thank you and goodbye to Carol and Mike and left around 10:00 a.m., riding south towards the village of Hungerford.

(Carol & Mike, Wantage, Oxfordshire)

I had a steep hill to walk and push the bike up right away, and found out that the upper inside area of my left knee hurt quite a bit. I rode slowly down into Hungerford on a very overcast day again, and then turned west and took the A4 into Marlborough. Marlborough turned out to be a very pretty town and it's my favorite of the trip so far.

I then continued west, passing by the Avebury ruins as my knee hurt too much to go off the highway and up a hill to see them. I was walking every hill, as I could only pedal on level and downhill stretches. The next town I came to west of Avebury was

89

Caine. Just outside the town I stopped and had an order of chips (French fries) and a glass of milk for 32 pence. In Caine I saw some ancient burial mounds and a Roman road that went back in the direction towards Avebury, and bought an apple, orange and banana for 28 pence for lunch - saving the orange for later.

On the road west again between Caine and Chippenham it began raining, and eventually I made it all the way into Bath on the A4. I pushed the bike up a huge hill to the YHA Youth Hostel to look into finding a place to spend the night. The Hostel Manager wanted 2 pounds, 20 pence for bed and breakfast, 40 pence for a sheet roll and 5 pounds, 10 pence for a temporary membership card. I told him thank you very much, but that it was too expensive for me - so I rode down the hill and turned west - in the general direction towards Wells.

I rode west out of Bath on the A39 and eventually I stopped at a huge, old house with lots of land surrounding it, and asked if I could camp on the property for the night. The elderly gentleman and his wife said I could sleep under a porch overhang to stay dry for the night. I set up my things and when they retired into the house for the evening, I walked a mile down the road for dinner at the New Inn. I had a glass of Courage beer, a glass of milk, fried chicken, chips, peas and two orders of bread for 1 pound, 71 pence.

Then I walked back to the house, recorded the day's events here in the log and watched it rain. Right now it's raining and dark, so I'm going to bed exhausted. Both knees hurt now, with the difference being that I can't walk very well on my right knee and I can't ride very well with my left knee, you figure it out! Now I'm going to bed...

(Colonel H. & Mrs. K., Marksbury, Bath)

~~~~~~~~~~

2018 Editorial Comment: Sleeping in my sleeping bag on the straw overnight with the shelter of a roof overhead, and the bonus of a shower and breakfast is one of the nicest experiences in life when given to you, and I really appreciated Carol and Mike's hospitality that morning - really amazing, especially as it was a gift concerning the condition I was in. I was already sore that morning from my first real day on the road the day before and their generosity was exactly what I needed to start this day.

The overcast skies really put a damper on the morning. There's something to be said for riding in cool, dry weather, but the introduction of wind and cold rain is not a pleasant experience. Marlborough was a very nice and scenic town that I especially enjoyed, and as I continued west I ran into knee issues that really challenged me, forcing me to walk every hill and pedal with only one leg doing most of the work on level and downhill stretches. The rain returned on the way towards Bath and by now it was almost an expected part of the day.

Bath was interesting from the perspective of seeing all the historic buildings, but it was very busy and when I located a youth hostel it turned out to be on top of the city's largest hill, of course, which was nearly impossible for me to reach the top in my condition. Once I actually made it to the top, it was such a disappointment to learn how much money they wanted to stay there. It just wasn't possible on my budget so I had to keep going, but at least the way out of town started out all downhill.

I figured I'd head towards Wells next and rode west out of Bath towards Marksbury on the A39 hoping to find a farm to camp on and eventually came across this really historic looking house and property, and the elderly couple agreed to my sleeping on their stone porch under a small roof overhang. I suggested it as a way to at least have some sort of roof over me in case it rained that night - which it did. It seemed rain was something I'd just have to get used to on this trip and one of the reasons I always say that adventures have a mind of their own, as you never know what will happen once you head down the winding road.

Walking down the road without my bike a mile to the New Inn for dinner was actually an enjoyable stroll, as it gave me a chance to help loosen and stretch my legs a bit so they wouldn't cramp up, while not stressing my knees very much. These two days had really put a lot of stress on my body and at this point I was still a long way from being a road hardened adventurer, as I was still breaking my body in to this life on the road. Even sleeping on the ground is something to get used to, as it gives you a good number of aches and pains in the morning without an air mattress, and riding stresses everything from your neck and shoulders, arms, rib muscles from pulling on the handlebars and of course the legs from the hips down. At least I celebrated the day with a very nice pub meal and a pint of Courage beer!

~~~~~~~~~~

Chapter Six - Bath, North East Somerset, to Wells, Somerset, and Christchurch, Dorset

~~~~~~~~~~

Saturday, June 9, 1979   Day 12

90 Miles | Total: 490 Miles

0 pounds, 44 pence | Total: 127 pounds, 61 pence

~~~~~~~~~~

It rained all night long and I didn't really sleep very well while lying on the rough, stone sidewalk. I had a thin foam pad under my sleeping bag, but it didn't help much. At least I was dry. I continue to dream like crazy at night these days.

After getting up at 8:30 a.m., I knocked on the Colonel & Mrs. K.'s front door. The lady of the house answered the door and started fixing breakfast. I took a long walk through the gardens and grounds with the Colonel. The estate was originally built in the 14th Century and was used as a monastery before it was finally completed in the 17th Century. After a breakfast of scrambled eggs, toast, cereal and coffee, I had a long, hot bath. My knees hurt a lot and the rest of me was very sore as well, and I'm sure sleeping on the stone sidewalk didn't help much after yesterday's ride, either.

After saying thank you and goodbye to Colonel & Mrs. K., I rode southwest on the A39 to Wells, and spent some time walking the grounds and taking a few pictures of the Cathedral.

Then I rode east on the A361 to Shepton, where I bought two apples, two bananas and an orange for 44 pence. I ate everything except for an apple to save for later and then continued my way southeast towards Bruton. It was very hilly in this area and I had to walk most of the hills because my knees hurt. It was an overcast day, however, it didn't rain - and the sun did come out a few times.

In Bruton, I stopped at a house and asked for water and was allowed to use the bathroom, and also enjoyed a cup of tea and was given directions. Then it was on to Gillingham and Shaftesbury, and later - right before I got to Blandford Forum - I was given some water, directions and eight cookies by an elderly woman. It was still light out so I kept on riding, and turned east on the A31 into Wimborne.

Then I rode as fast as I could into Christchurch, even though I was extremely tired. A rising full moon helped light my way, and I made it to David and Jayne's house (Bet's nephew and girlfriend) at 10:00 p.m., just as the darkness was fully settled in. There was a festival going on in downtown Christchurch with thousands of people filling the streets, but somehow I made it through the crowds.

David fixed sandwiches and tea, and I had a glass of milk. I've got a huge craving for milk these days. I drink gallons of water which is very good for me, but calories are one area that I don't have to worry about these days. So far I've spent over six pounds over 12 days which has conserved my money, but this will probably not continue on for long. Next it's on to Paris. I must remember to write to Bruce (from our 8,111 mile bicycle adventure in 1976-1977) from Paris, as we always wanted to continue our original bicycle adventure to Europe. I can't stay awake any longer now, so good night.

~~~~~~~~~~~

2018 Editorial Comment: This was such a long day and seemed to just never end, but at least it had a happy ending. I never considered riding all the way to Christchurch in one day, but I'd decided with all the rain Southern England was having, it made sense to head to the Continent and ride to Paris next to find some sunny weather. It seemed like a good plan to me at the time, but I didn't really understand how the weather across the South of England, the English Channel and Northern France was all interconnected. I just thought if it was cloudy and wet where I was, it must be sunny in France - right?

I hadn't slept very well on the stones of the Colonel and Mrs. K.'s porch, as I only had a thin foam pad underneath my hips and shoulders, but it did keep me dry as it rained all night long. Even though it was June, the temperatures weren't very warm at the time, so you can imagine the damp cold of the situation trying to sleep on the cold stones, but I was so tired I slept regardless with my mind oversaturated with dreams. The fact that everything is new, difficult and challenging on adventures, stimulates the mind, especially the subconscious, and stirs up new thoughts and connections to everything going on in your life - past, present and future. At least that's my theory.

I really wish I could have given everyone who helped me out on this trip full credit within the context of the story at least, as I've had to omit everyone's last name and their house name/street number due to the times we live in today, even though the events happened 39 years ago almost to the day now. Even with the passing of time though one can't be too sure, and omitting some of the details doesn't detract from the hospitality and graciousness everyone extended to me during my adventure.

The Colonel and I had a nice walk through the grounds and gardens of the property that morning as the lady of the house began preparing breakfast, which was such a privilege for me to be part of as they were both elderly and the property was such a historic feature going back to the 14th Century. The Colonel explained the history of the property through the years and then I was treated to a wonderful breakfast and a hot bath! The bath did wonders to restore some sense of function to my body after a tough day and night, especially my knees and joints from the damp and cold. What a blessing it all was!

After saying thank you and goodbye to the Colonel and Mrs. K., I rode down to Wells and took in the amazing sight of the cathedral from the wide expanse of the lawn and grounds in front of it. There were pockets of tourists here and there on the grounds, and I parked my bike and sat on the lawn for a while just taking it all in - I was actually in England and seeing history before my eyes! Then I took a few pictures of the front facade with all the statues and took a look inside.

After Wells, I rode towards Christchurch where I planned to take the ferry to Le Havre, France, for my journey to Paris. The day kept going on and on, and I had no idea I'd eventually make it all the way to Christchurch, but I didn't find a good stopping place along the way and ended up riding in the dark into Christchurch. At least the terrain was relatively flat and the sun set quite late in the day, as the Summer Solstice was less than two weeks away.

I'd toured London with David and Jayne during my stay at Bet's house in Farnham Common, and they'd told me to stop by when I found myself in Christchurch, so I did just that. Even though it was 10:00 p.m. when I arrived, the entire town was alive with a street festival filling the entire downtown area. They took me in like a long, lost relative and it was just what I needed, as the day had taken quite a toll on my body - actually the past few days.

The simple offering of food and shelter to a traveler on the road, and the receiving of such generosity, is one of the most basic of human conditions, and was such a blessing to me at the time. While the weather wasn't the best for bicycling through Southern England and my body was feeling the strain of the past few days' worth of efforts, I was experiencing a very special time in my life as people were caring for me throughout the trip so far, forever endearing me to the people of the British Isles...

~~~~~~~~~~

Christchurch, Dorset

~~~~~~~~~~

Sunday, June 10, 1979   Day 13

30 Miles | Total: 520 Miles

0 pounds, 0 pence | Total: 127 pounds, 61 pence

~~~~~~~~~~

This morning I felt like I had been hit by a truck - but at the same time it felt very good - however that could be. David got up around 9:00 a.m. and I got up at 10:00 a.m. After a breakfast of Corn Flakes, toast and coffee, David left to go get Jayne prior to going over to his brother's house. I took a shower and examined my aching legs and knees, and pronounced that they would live with a little rest. Then I walked around downtown Christchurch and saw the ruins, the church and what was left over from last night's festival. Some folk dancers were here and there, and it was yet another overcast day, but it hadn't rained yet.

Then David, Jayne, Colin and Julie drove by and saw me walking down the street on my walking tour of Christchurch, and stopped to pick me up. We had a beer and listened to some guys singing folk songs to a small crowd of 50 or so people outdoors in a courtyard. Then we drove over to David's brother's house and had a big chicken dinner. After dinner we watched England vs. Sweden playing soccer on TV. It was a scoreless game in the end. After the soccer match we watched a Bing Crosby film, *A Connecticut Yankee in King Arthur's Court.*

I have continued to notice small differences between British and American lifestyles while on this trip:

- *For dinner the British don't seem to have the same habit of setting the table for dinner with individual napkins at each place setting.*

- *Drinks aren't often served with the meal, which must be due to all the tea and coffee that is consumed during the day.*

- *There are many differences in housing, mannerisms, social customs and the like, but at the same time most everything is pretty much the same as I'm used to. Life is still life and people are still people wherever you go. I have enjoyed England very much except for the weather.*

It started raining again, and after more coffee and biscuits over at David's brother's house we came back home to David's house. There we had more tea and sandwiches, and watched the telly. David's parents came home from their trip, where they were helping to decorate the upstairs of Bet's house. Immediately we had more coffee, biscuits, milk, cheese and crackers. The British do love to snack! All for now.

~~~~~~~~~~~

2018 Editorial Comment: After starting out the day feeling like I'd been run over by a truck and pronouncing that I'd live with a little rest, it turned out to be a most enjoyable day. After breakfast, I strolled through Christchurch and took in all the sights and sounds of the morning following the big festival, which was another opportunity and moment of quiet reflection for me to realize I really was in England after all!

It was an opportune moment when David, Jayne, Colin and Julie drove by and saw me during my walking tour, and an enjoyable time having a pint and listening to folk music. The visit with everyone at David's brother's house was really nice with the big meal and the soccer match on the telly, while the Bing Crosby film was excellent, as the novel by Mark Twain has always been one of my favorite books.

I couldn't help but notice small differences between the British and American way of life at the time, or at least my experiences growing up, which was all part of my immersion into British culture that I'd never experienced before. Of course, 1979 was a completely different time than today in 2018, but everything was new to me at the time and I kept jotting down small insights that came to me in my logbook when they occurred to me - sort of a time capsule of my thoughts.

The day's logbook entry finishes with a little sketch of the Eiffel Tower and the saying *Onward to France!* Yet, I had no idea what I was getting myself into with my desire to see the Continent. For the most part, it's always best to not know the future and what it holds, for then we wouldn't be able to enjoy the moment knowing what was ahead of us for better or worse. I was simply enjoying being in Christchurch with David and Jayne, Colin and Julie, and Mr. and Mrs. B., and looked forward to the adventure across the English Channel waiting for me.

~~~~~~~~~~

~~~~~~~~~~

Monday, June 11, 1979   Day 14

0 Miles | Total: 520 Miles

0 pounds, 0 pence | Total: 127 pounds, 61 pence

~~~~~~~~~~

Today was another day of rest. I got up around 10:00 a.m. when Mrs. B. woke me up and then I took a shower. She had breakfast all ready for me which included 2 fried eggs, toast, cereal, bacon and coffee. I've been lucky to have had breakfast and a bath or a shower each day of the trip so far. I did a load of laundry and then put it out on the line to dry. Mrs. B. went to work at noon and I took a walk down to the beach. The beach reminded me of the old days at the Sea Gun Resort Hotel in Texas. I walked up and down the beach and enjoyed the mild and sunny day. The beach looked like Florida with all of the people lying out in the sun.

From the beach I returned to the house and Mr. B. came home from work around 2:00 p.m. We watched some telly and had a late dinner with Colin, Julie, David, Jayne and Mr. & Mrs. B. Dinner was lamb ribs, peas, potatoes, cooked tomato, broccoli hearts, pudding and peaches - very nice. After dinner we watched telly, looked at a family slide show of the kids when they were younger, and munched on biscuits and cakes with coffee.

I feel fine now after two days of rest. Tomorrow I'll catch a ferry to France.

(Mr. & Mrs. B., David, Jayne, Collin, Julie, Christchurch, Dorset)

~~~~~~~~~~~

2018 Editorial Comment: This was another much needed day of rest for me after the marathon ride two days earlier. I'd stressed my knees and probably every other part of my body that day, as jumping right into three days of hard riding from an almost standstill was really too much. At least I felt good about heading to France the next day, while not knowing ahead of time how things would turn out on the Continent for me.

Mr. and Mrs. B.'s return from Bet's house the night before reconnected me full circle to the wonderful first few days of the trip, and the exceptional tour of London with David and Jayne. They had accepted me as part of the family and it was really enjoyable to see the family slides when the kids were growing up. Those slides, which showed Great Britain during an earlier time, were in and of themselves an interesting observation of how life had changed over the past twenty years.

I really enjoyed my stroll along the beach, and it was full of sunbathers and people strolling along the water's edge. I'd never grown up around the ocean and walking along the beach was always a special time for me no matter where it was. Looking out across the English Channel towards France also allowed me to anticipate the next leg of my trip, as I had no idea what to expect the next day after boarding the ferry.   Would I find better weather? Could I communicate with people in France? I had an English-French dictionary with me that I hoped would help me bridge the language gap, as I didn't speak French. After all, this was an adventure I was on and while it had been quite nice and civilized so far, I was willing to find out what France held for me, as I'd always wanted to see Europe. I'd find out soon enough...

~~~~~~~~~~

Chapter Seven - Christchurch, Dorset, U.K., to Paris, France, to Newington, Nr. Folkestone, Kent, England, U.K.

~~~~~~~~~~

The Longest Day

(Summary)

Tuesday, June 12, 1979 through Thursday, June 14, 1979

Days 15, 16, 17

~~~~~~~~~~

Tuesday, Day 15

25 Miles from Christchurch to the Port of Southampton

Wednesday, Day 16

117 Miles on the Ferry from Christchurch to Le Havre, France

70 Miles riding from Le Havre to Rouen

85 Miles from Rouen to Paris by train

20 Miles walking and riding through Paris

188 Miles from Paris to Dunkerque by train

Thursday, Day 17

100 Miles from Dunkerque to Dover (3 Crossings)

20 Miles from Dover towards Ashford

625 Miles | Total: 1,145 Miles

~~~~~~~~~~

Tuesday - 13 pounds, 97 pence

Wednesday - 24 pounds, 50 pence

Thursday - 11 pounds, 50 pence

49 pounds, 97 pence | Total: 177 pounds, 58 pence

~~~~~~~~~~

25 Miles

13 pounds, 97 pence

Today I woke up at about 10:00 a.m. again, showered and ate breakfast which included two fried eggs, toast, cereal, ham and coffee. I hope that I'll have good luck in France. I had everything packed up and ready by noon, and Mrs. B. gave me directions to get started and I drew out a small map based on her description. I then said thank you and goodbye to Mrs. B., and rode northeast to Lyndhurst. I met a guy named Azhar along the way and then continued on to the Port of Southampton, where I bought my ferry ticket to Le Havre, France, for 12 pounds 20 pence. At that point, I had lots of extra time on my hands and walked around the port area of Southampton for a while in the rain.

I had lunch at a Wimpy Burger restaurant - double burger, fries and a milkshake (more like chocolate milk) for 1 pound 38 pence. The food wasn't very good at all. I had a craving for a hamburger, but I really don't know why. I should have had some fruit instead.

Afterwards, I walked around some more and stopped in at a gas station to use the bathroom. I bought a cup of coffee for 15 pence (estimate) and talked to the guy that worked there for a while, and then went back down to the ferry terminal to wait. There weren't any people around the terminal, so I got out my English-French dictionary and read all 1,000 words with French translations. While waiting for the ferry I spent 24 pence on a Milky Way candy bar and a glass of milk.

The ferry leaves at 11:00 p.m. and it's 7:30 p.m. now. I wrote down the lyrics for two songs in my logbook to pass the time. It's been overcast for all but one and a half days that I've been in England, so maybe it's a good idea to go to France next. I hope they have sunshine. If I had wanted to see clouds, I could have just as well stayed in Seattle, and the weather would have probably been better there too. So now that the logbook is caught up, it's on to France tomorrow - hope for good luck!

~~~~~~~~~~

2018 Editorial Comment: Mr. and Mrs. B. had been so nice to me there in Christchurch and I'd really appreciated the effort everyone had gone through to take care of me - again a perfect stranger being welcomed into the family. Simply amazing.

I tried to put on a brave face for my trip to France, but I knew I didn't speak French and had heard stories of how travelers could have difficulties overseas when they didn't speak the language. I knew I would need help from regular folks to camp out on farms and hoped there was some way of sorting out how to make it work out. Studying my English-French dictionary there in the ferry terminal actually made me a bit nervous, as I had time on my hands to think and really didn't understand the French language or how to pronounce it at all. Eventually I had to just put the dictionary away and find another way to pass the time until boarding the ferry.

The Wimpy Burger meal had been a big disappointment, as I was hungry and wanted a satisfying meal. After that, snacking at the terminal for something to eat was my only option. I was glad I made it to the ferry terminal in plenty of time, as one never knows when traveling by bike, but the waiting felt like it was endless and all I wanted to do was go to sleep...

~~~~~~~~~~~

Wednesday, June 13, 1979   Day 16

480 Miles

195 francs at 4 francs to the dollar = 49 dollars total

49 dollars = 24 pounds, 50 pence

(Note: I'll add my Editorial Comments within the text of the logbook entries in France in order to stay within the context of the story.)

Logbook Entry: I didn't get very much sleep last night on the ferry and even though the seats looked nice, they weren't very comfortable. This morning I spent 5 francs on breakfast: cereal, coffee and tea. I got off the ferry at 6:30 a.m., and pushed the bike into town for a little while to get used to my new surroundings as the city was still asleep here in Le Havre.

Today was very overcast again, and as I left Le Havre and rode into Tancarville it started raining again. It continued to rain all the way into Lillebonne, where I bought an apple, pear and a banana for 3.5 francs. From there I rode on into Caudebec-en-Caux - again in the rain of course - and then continued on into Duclair. From there it really started pouring down rain as I continued on into Rouen, very cold and wet.

~~~~~~~~~~

2018 Editorial Comment: I'd ridden 65 miles at that point and was feeling like I'd jumped out of the frying pan and into the fire so to speak, with all the terrible weather I'd found in France - much worse than it had been in England. I was cold, wet and hungry,

109

and already tired from riding the day before and not sleeping on the ferry. I loved the French countryside and wanted to really make this leg of my adventure work out, but found that I couldn't communicate with anyone just as I'd been afraid of.

Along the way I'd stopped to talk to an elderly woman in front of her farmhouse to ask her if I could get some water for my water bottle. She didn't seem to understand what I wanted and didn't offer anything in reply as I'm sure she didn't speak any English. My attempts at translating fell flat as they probably didn't drink tap water in France. In retrospect, I'm sure they only drank bottled water. As a result, she had no idea what I was asking for and really only gave me a blank look of not understanding, so I rode on.

I was able to take a nice photo of my bike in front of some sort of beautiful château along the way and I really wished I could have somehow connected with the French people. The fruit vendor who sold me the fruit didn't speak a word of English to me and my experiences told me this would be very rough going if I couldn't speak to anyone. I couldn't afford to stay in hotels, so my only option was to take a train into Paris to at least say I'd been there and seen it.

If I had only been able to speak French, I'm sure I would have loved my visit to France. I didn't hold anyone but myself responsible for the outcome of this leg of my adventure, as it was my deficiency for not speaking French and not the people's issue that they didn't speak English. I knew I'd be missing out on the French countryside I loved, but at this point I couldn't do anything about it...

~~~~~~~~~

<u>Logbook Entry</u>: I decided at that point to go down to the train station and catch a train into Paris. I had already experienced the fact that I couldn't talk to anyone in France - 1,000 word English-French dictionary or not - and I wasn't having a good time in the cold and rain. At one point, I tried to simply ask an older woman in a rural house for some water, and it was almost impossible to get her to understand my question. Paris might be better. I spent 37 francs for a ticket to Paris and 13 francs for a ticket for my bike. I carried my sleeping bag with me on the train, but left the other bags on the bike. I was a little worried about them, but I knew the bike was in the baggage car just behind my car. On the train I spent 4.5 francs for two candy bars, and got off the train in Paris.

The weather was quite a bit better in Paris, and although it was still overcast, it wasn't raining. I helped show another guy where the baggage car was and picked up my bike. I rode over to the Eiffel Tower and saw as many sights as I could, even though it was at times very hard to maneuver my bike through the crowded streets of Paris. I spent 5 francs on some more fruit - an apple, banana and an orange. It became very clear that there wouldn't be a place for me to spend the night in Paris. I had checked the price of a run-down looking hotel and found out that every place in the city would be out of my price range. As I stood on a crowded side street, I made a decision. France was not a good idea for me on this trip, as I just couldn't communicate with anyone here. So I decided that Holland sounded like a better idea, as it was flat, had a lot of bicycles and the people for the most part spoke English - or at least I had been told that.

~~~~~~~~~~

<u>2018 Editorial Comment</u>: I took a photo of my bike in front of the Eiffel Tower in order to prove I'd been there and it remains today one of my favorite photos as I've used it for the cover of this *Book Nine*. I didn't go up into the Eiffel Tower and saw the outside of The Louvre, visited the Act de Triomphe, rode along the Seine, saw Notre-Dame de Paris (Notre Dame Cathedral) and many other sites in the heart of Paris.

While I loved Paris just as much as I had London (in fact they both remain my favorite cities to this day), I knew I couldn't stay due to both the language issues and my lack of funds, so it was time to make a new decision and head towards Holland. Another reason why I always say that adventures have a mind of their own and you never know what you're in for once you travel down the winding road...

~~~~~~~~~~

<u>Logbook Entry</u>: So I rode over to my original train station, the Guar de Nord (the north train station) looking for a train to Dunkerque, but found out that I had to ride across town to a different station, the Guar de l'Est. So off I went, beginning to feel quite tired and disappointed in this trip to the Continent by now. At the next station I bought a ticket to Dunkerque for 109 francs and another 13 francs for the bike. I was told to take all the bags off of the bike and I was left holding six bike bags in all as I boarded the train. I rode first class with a Japanese guy who was a dancer living in France and a girl from Washington D.C. The train left at 9:30 p.m. and was scheduled to arrive in Dunkerque at 12:45 a.m. I spent 5 francs on the train for a candy bar and a soda, and made my plan to ride on to Amsterdam after Dunkerque.

~~~~~~~~~~

2018 Editorial Comment: By the time I arrived in Dunkerque, I had been up for almost two full days (Christchurch to Southampton and Le Havre to Paris to Dunkerque). I was very tired, but hadn't been able to sleep on either the ferry or the train. I'd ridden well over a hundred miles on this individual leg of the trip, in addition to all my walking and riding through Paris (estimated at 20 miles), and I was exhausted.

Hand carrying my six bike bags was very tedious and difficult to even make my way into the first class section of the train, which I believe was my only option when purchasing my ticket. I knew I'd spent a fortune so far on this leg of my trip and at this point I just wanted to get to Holland where I could finally talk to someone. While we had a little conversation there on the train, it was late and everyone was tired during the evening train ride and just tried to sleep.

~~~~~~~~~~

Thursday, June 14, 1979   Day 17

120 Miles

84 francs = 21 dollars

1 pound = 2 dollars

23 dollars total = 11 pounds, 50 pence

Logbook Entry: When the train stopped in Dunkerque in the middle of the night at 12:45 a.m., I was the only one to get off the train. I felt at the time that I was stepping off of the train and into a black and white WWII movie. There was only a small, old brick building with a single bare light bulb burning outside it in the cold mist and fog that swirled around everything. It looked like a train switching yard, all in shades of black and gray, dirty and grimy as if untouched for 40 years, with overhead wires, large coarse crushed rock and tracks dimly illuminated in the cold, misty fog of the night.

I was tired and cold and walked about 30 yards while carrying my six unwieldy bike bags to the little shack of a building, and tried to explain to an old man there that I was looking to claim my bike from the baggage car. He didn't speak English and I didn't speak French - and through sign language and by my pointing to an old bike in the corner of the building he finally understood me. He told me in French that my bike wasn't there and was still on the train, while pointing at the train - or at least that's what I understood. That's when I started to panic...

In that moment, the train slowly began moving into the darkness and cold mist of this surrealistic setting I'd found myself in, and I ran full of desperation and a lot of effort with my six bike bags in hand swinging wildly as the train slowly pulled away. I jumped on the steps of one of the last cars of the train and climbed the steps to where I was able to stand in the connecting area of a second class car where the rest rooms were located as the train picked up speed.

~~~~~~~~~~

2018 Editorial Comment: Only one other time, much later in my life, have I been in such a surreal experience as I had been getting off the train in the middle of the night with my bike bags in hand, feeling like I'd stepped back in time into the scene and setting of a WWII movie. It was actually a little frightening at the time, because everything was wrong and there was no place to accept departing passengers or anything. I was in a grimy switching yard with multiple train tracks with nothing but dirty chunks of rock scattered across all the track rails.

The sign over the old brick building, that hadn't seen repairs for decades, had said Dunkerque where the train stopped in front of it, so it was my stop - wasn't it? My concern was to not become separated from my bike, but here I was in the little building with an old man who didn't speak English and my bike was nowhere to be seen.

What was I to do but run for the train once it started moving? It was such an awkward moment, trying to run with six bike bags in hand across a thirty yard stretch of grimy broken rock and multiple wires strung overhead, but I made it to one of the last cars of the train and jumped onto the steps, not knowing if I was going to kill myself in the process. Luckily, I was able to get into the foyer area where the rest rooms were located as the train made its way to - where?

~~~~~~~~~~

Logbook Entry: After about 20 miles we arrived at the Dunkerque Marine Terminal and I got off and went to the baggage area. My bike wasn't there. They said that the bike must still be on the train and that it was being loaded onto the ferry to Dover - so I bought a ticket for the 2 a.m. ferry and they said I could look for the bike once everything was loaded on board the ferry. Here I was, the second night in a row without sleep, boarding a 2:00 a.m. ferry to Dover having no idea where my bike was.

I was able to get help from Evon, the ferry's purser who spoke both English and French, after discovering that my bike wasn't on the ferry. We looked in all of the baggage cars and there was no bike to be found. Evon refunded my ticket and said that I wouldn't be allowed to get off the ferry in Dover, and instead would have to make the return trip back to Dunkerque because my bike must still be there.

I tried but failed to get any sleep on the two and a half hour ferry trip to Dover, and then we turned around and sailed again for Dunkerque. I arrived very tired in Dunkerque at 9:00 a.m. and Evon took me on the employee bus to the train station in Dunkerque. My bike was there!

My fun meter was pegged by that time, so I decided to go back to England, rain or no rain. At least there I didn't have any troubles. Evon persuaded the driver of the employee bus to take me back to the Marine Terminal and there I picked up my bike bags where I had left them.

I went into the waiting area to change my shirt, shave and brush my teeth. I still felt dirty, even though my pants and shoes had finally dried out from the rains of the day before. I met a French girl, who was also waiting for the ferry, but she spoke only a few words of English, and about the only thing that I can say in French is Merci. So here I am. I bought a ferry ticket to Dover for 84 francs, and I'm feeling cold, tired and I'm starving.

When the time came that I could finally get back on the ferry to Dover, I met some Americans from Washington DC, Portland and Seattle. I was thirsty and hungry, so I bought three small Cokes for 60 pence and a very large and sweet candy bar for 40 pence. I was so tired that I could hardly stay awake any longer, and on this trip across the English Channel the weather had changed for the worse.

This was a much smaller ferry than I had been used to, and the winds became very strong and the channel was very rough with large waves throwing the boat around. Between the Cokes and the chocolate bar, I wasn't feeling very well. I'm sure that I was turning green as I tried to hold onto the railing around the bar. A bottle slid about ten feet down the bar as the ferry pitched up, and when I tried to get to the bathroom it was like leaping for the other side of the boat and attempting to grasp a hold of something - anything.

I got sick big time in the bathroom and it was even hard to aim for the toilet as the ship was moving so much, and the confined space made my seasickness worse. At this point things weren't looking very good at all. The ordeal at sea continued on and on, and after what seemed like ages I got off the boat in Dover with a very large headache.

~~~~~~~~~~

<u>2018 Editorial Comment</u>:   I was hurtin' for certain on this final ferry ride of the longest day. I hadn't slept for two nights in a row and was beyond being exhausted. I'd finally found my bike again with the help of Evon the ferry's purser - who was literally an angel, for without his help I would have lost my bike. Evon went above and beyond to solve the mystery of my missing bike and had to do everything within his power to convince the driver of the employee bus for the ferry company to drive me both ways to the train station and back to the port.

How I missed my proper station exit to retrieve my bike in the first place I'll never know, because there was never a proper Dunkerque train station that I ever saw or was aware of. All I know, is that without Evon's help this would have become a major disaster for me and to this day I'm forever grateful to him for saving the day and my adventure!

I'd had little to eat during this bicycling, and train and ferry riding odyssey of crossing the English Channel four times in total. In fact, I hadn't had much of anything to eat besides some fruit, sodas and chocolate bars since leaving Christchurch, and my stomach was set up for disaster on my third ferry crossing between Dunkerque and Dover.

This ferry was miniature compared to the other channel ferries I'd ridden on, and it figured that the seas and winds would be fierce during this final crossing. I'd never seen a ship pitch up and down, and side to side, like that one had and everyone was hanging on for dear life - and of course my stomach couldn't take it. I was a wobbly mess by the time I got off the ferry in Dover, yet *The Longest Day* was far from over...

~~~~~~~~~~

Logbook Entry: The white cliffs of Dover were very pretty as we approached the Port of Dover and the ferry terminal, and the sky was still overcast and it was very windy. I rode uphill into the wind on the A20 into Folkestone and then on towards Ashford. About halfway towards Ashford I stopped in at a farmhouse for water and the lady of the house came to the door with a paintbrush in her hand. She said that I could sleep in their small barn and then fixed me toast, a poached egg with tomato and a cookie.

I met her daughter Heather who was about 14 and her son Matthew who was 17 when they came back from school. I didn't meet Margaret's other son John, but I met her husband Ian when he came in from fencing out in the fields. I watched the movie *Paper Chase* on telly and then took a long bath. They invited me to have a dinner of fish and chips, and peas - as well as peaches and ice cream smothered in fresh cream for dessert. Then I stayed up until midnight talking with Ian and Margaret after the kids had gone to bed. Now here I am in the barn and it's time for my first good night's sleep in days. The longest day had finally come to an end and it's finally time to sleep.

~~~~~~~~~~

2018 Editorial Comment: I thought I'd died and gone to Heaven when Margaret let me stay on their farm and treated me like family. I really hadn't slept since the night in Christchurch before riding to Southampton to catch the first ferry to Le Havre. The bath, watching a favorite movie of mine, enjoying a wonderful meal and our conversation that evening, and then finally sleeping in the barn were all so rejuvenating for me, as I was about to collapse on the side of the road without their heartfelt hospitality. I have no idea how I stayed up until midnight talking with Ian and Margaret there in the living room that evening, but I was on Cloud 9 just to be able to know there was finally an end to my *Longest Day!*

I didn't allow my difficulties in France to detract from my love for Paris or the countryside, as my language issues were my own and no one else's fault, and Evon's assistance had been a real blessing to me, a complete stranger to him. However, it was this joy I felt on my arrival in England that I'll cherish forever when Margaret offered me comfort and shelter from the storm of the past three days during my endless travels. She was literally an angel!

I loved the delicious food Margaret served as I was literally starving, but hadn't told her that, and it was such a comfort to be taken care of in my time of need. The *Paper Chase* film is one of my all-time favorite movies, and talking with Ian and Margaret and the kids was really special, as were all my discussions with families across the U.K.

It was such a stimulating time in my life with all the challenges and difficulties I was experiencing, while at the same time all the joys of meeting new people and being welcomed into their families and being so well taken care of. Everything about being part of such a long hoped for adventure, and seeing and experiencing everything new overseas, was washing over and through me like a wave and making me new again.

This odyssey had been the longest three full days of my life and my longest time ever without the opportunity for some proper sleep. Whenever I've faced difficult challenges in life I've always looked back on this time as my trial by fire - for if I could survive *The Longest Day,* I could survive anything. This knowledge would serve me well over the course of my life as my challenges never lessened throughout the years but only grew larger and ever more difficult, and knowing I could survive this journey gave me the confidence that I could survive anything.

While I hadn't asked for this lesson from *The School of Hard Knocks,* I now understand it was one of the most important and valuable lessons I've learned in my life...

~~~~~~~~~~

Newington, Nr. Folkestone, Kent

~~~~~~~~~~

Friday, June 15, 1979   Day 18

30 Miles | Total: 1,175 Miles

3 pounds, 40 pence | Total: 180 pounds, 98 pence

~~~~~~~~~~

Matthew woke me up in the barn at 7:00 a.m. and at the time I was sleeping like a log. I got dressed and had a breakfast of tea, toast, cereal, bacon and eggs, and baked beans. Matthew and I then caught the bus at 7:40 a.m. (1 pound, 45 pence for the round trip ticket) and rode from the Newington Forge bus stop into Canterbury together where Matthew goes to school. I spent the morning and early afternoon walking around the town and visited the beautiful Canterbury Cathedral. For lunch I had fish and chips with coffee for a total of 1 pound, 53 pence including the tip. Later for dessert I bought an apple turnover for 12 pence, a newspaper for 10 pence and a Coke to quench my thirst for 20 pence.

It rained on and off in town, and then in the afternoon I took the bus back to the house getting off again at the Newington Forge stop. I waited in the barn for the thunderstorm to pass for ten minutes and at that time Margaret returned home from shopping. She invited me in and then she had to leave on another errand, so I played the piano for an hour or so until she returned again with Heather. We had tea and donuts, and then Heather had to go upstairs to study. Margaret had to run another errand, so I sat down at the kitchen table to write this entry in the logbook and played the piano.

We all had a late dinner after watching *All Creatures Great and Small* on the telly. Dinner was pork chops, potatoes, gravy, corn, tea, rolls, ice cream and bananas. We talked until about 11:00 p.m. and then I went out to the shed for a good night's sleep.

(Ian & Margaret, John 19, Matthew 17, Heather 14, Newington, Nr. Folkestone, Kent)

~~~~~~~~~~

2018 Editorial Comment: This was such a great day visiting the historic town of Canterbury with its amazing cathedral and narrow streets. It started off being woken up from one of the deepest sleeps I'm sure I'd had in a long, long time, needing to make up for time lost over the previous three days. It was fine though, as we'd made the plan the night before for me to ride the bus with Matthew and it was shocking how quickly the morning arrived!

One of the best experiences in life is when you know you're being taken care of in some way, when recent experience had given you quite a different feeling. This journey was such an emotional time of high and low points within the context of just being alive, and while we often go through our days without any specific stimulus sort of on autopilot, adventure wakes us up and makes us feel every part of what being alive really means, both good and bad.

My two sessions of playing the piano that day went a long way towards my rediscovering the joy of sitting down at the keyboard, making yet another attempt to understand the instrument and try to play something spontaneously without music. While I wouldn't break the code as far as being able to write songs as a songwriter during these sessions, I would try again in a music store later on in this trip as well. It wouldn't be until I returned to Michigan State University in 1980 and discovered the piano practice rooms in the basement of the College of Music, that I'd make progress in this musical endeavor of mine - and it still wouldn't be until Advent 1989 that I'd actually begin writing my own songs.

After another wonderful dinner, watching *All Creatures Great and Small* on the telly was another special joy for me, as I'd earlier wanted to become a veterinarian, and the TV series about Dr. Herriot and his adventures in North Yorkshire was a favorite of mine to watch. I grew up reading all the books and watching the show on TV, so this was a real privilege to see it with Ian, Margaret and family. Another opportunity to talk late into the evening really capped this day off in a special way for me and then I settled in for another satisfying night's sleep in the barn.

~~~~~~~~~~

Chapter Eight - Newington, Nr. Folkestone, Kent, to Guildford, Surrey

~~~~~~~~~~

Saturday, June 16, 1979   Day 19

100 Miles | Total: 1,275 Miles

0 pounds, 80 pence | Total: 181 pounds, 78 pence

~~~~~~~~~~

I was up and dressed by 8:00 a.m., even though I thought I'd slept until 11:00 a.m. I had a breakfast of eggs, sausage, toast, cereal and tea with the family, and then said thank you and goodbye to Ian and John, who I'd since met, as they were leaving the house. I took a bath, packed all my things together, and then said thank you and goodbye to Margaret and Heather.

I rode north to Ashford and then west to Biddenden on the A262 - where I bought an apple, orange and a banana for 30 pence. I stopped in a small town, and had an ice cream cone and two chocolate bars for 50 pence. I ate the ice cream cone in a park and was attacked by a swan that wanted the cone for itself instead. I rode on to Royal Tunbridge Wells and then on in the direction of East Grinstead on the A264.

Just prior to reaching East Grinstead in West Sussex, I stopped at a farm on the A264 for water and directions. A very pretty girl answered the door and her mother invited me in for tea. We talked for about 15 minutes over tea, telling me about her family and the work her husband does for a living, and then the lady of the house had to walk their black and yellow Labrador Retrievers, so I said thank you and goodbye, and rode on towards East Grinstead.

About a mile down the road, a motorcycle and I had a minor collision at an intersection, as he started to move forward prior to my bike having cleared his front tire. I had a small cut on my ankle and decided to take a break and maybe call it a day, so I returned to the farm I'd stopped at for more conversation and local directions for a place to camp. After our second conversation my leg felt a bit better and I decided it wasn't a show-stopper, so I decided to continue riding on. Once again I set off, this time without mishap, and rode into East Grinstead and then north to Godstone on the A22.

The weather was very good all day, with broken clouds and sunshine. The weather even cleared up nicer in the evening. I had been wearing shorts today, but with the sunset I could see that more clouds were headed my way. I continued on into Redhill, Reigate and Dorking - and then halfway to Guildford I found a farm with a barn to sleep in for the night. So at the moment I'm lying here in the straw, and finishing up writing the day's adventures. Good night.

~~~~~~~~~~~

2018 Editorial Comment: This had been a real up and down sort of day, and as I was feeling refreshed after my stay down towards Newington, I was able to put in a 100 mile day. The minor accident with the motorcycle when it ran into my wheel turned out to be less of a collision than it first appeared. My bike was fine as was his and the cut on my ankle wasn't as serious as it first looked.

On my earlier bicycle adventure around the U.S. with my friend Bruce, I had coined the *only friend in town* theory as someone to get advice from if you ran out of options, so I turned around and returned to the farm to ask for camping directions. We had a nice conversation and after the initial shock of having a collision with a motorcycle, I assessed it was too nice a day to call it quits for the day and kept riding on.

It turned out to be one of my best riding days ever, except for the incident with the motorcycle and the swan that attacked me trying to get my ice cream cone in the park - it failed by the way. So here I was at the end of the day and a long ride relaxing on the straw in a barn, relishing another day in England!

~~~~~~~~~~

Chapter Nine - Guildford, Surrey, to Farnham Common, Buckinghamshire

~~~~~~~~~~

Sunday, June 17, 1979   Day 20

50 Miles | Total: 1,325 Miles

1 pound, 5 pence | Total: 182 pounds, 83 pence

~~~~~~~~~~

I slept quite well on the straw in the open barn last night, as it was very clean and made for a nice place to sleep. I woke up early, probably around 7:00 a.m. and although it was an overcast morning it hadn't rained. I went back up to the farmhouse for water, which he gave me and thanked the man for letting me sleep in his barn.

I rode on to Guildford and was very hungry as I hadn't had lunch or dinner yesterday, and began to look for a place to eat breakfast. In the town of Guildford I saw a café that was open, but I had run out of pounds and it was a Sunday morning. The banks were all closed and all I had were U.S. traveler's checks. The manager of the café was nice enough to cash a traveler's check once I told him what the exchange rate was: 2.05. I was ready for a good meal and for breakfast I had an egg, fried toast, bacon, sausage, fried tomato, cereal, toast, jam and orange juice - and he charged me 1 pound, 5 pence including the tip.

After breakfast I rode north to Woking, and had a good talk with an older man who gave me directions and an AA map book. Then I rode northwest to Windsor Castle, but didn't go inside as there was no place to leave my bike and the tourists were swarming all around, so I just took a couple of photos of the mile long drive that led to the castle.

Eventually, I rode up to Slough and Farnham Common where I stopped in to see Bet and family again - the family that I had stayed with when I first arrived in England. They were on the back patio by the pool when I rode up and even though I asked for water - I was given a beer instead. Bet fixed me a couple of salad sandwiches and we talked for the afternoon. Bet did my laundry and we had dinner with some of their friends: steak pieces in gravy, mushrooms, potatoes, cauliflower, peas, strawberries and ice cream, chocolates, biscuits, cheese, celery, coffee - as well as gin and tonics. We all talked until midnight, and then Bet's friends left and everyone went to bed.

~~~~~~~~~~

2018 Editorial Comment: This was just a magical day as all the events unfolded, and after I finished writing this day's entry and went to bed, my logbook has an extra entry where I woke up again to draw some wizard sketches and then went back to sleep again. That shows how overstimulated my imagination was from all the many events that were happening to me on this trip.

I was starving again riding into Guildford and very much appreciated the café's owner cashing my traveler's check for me. At the time Windsor Castle was a disappointment for me, as the entire area was full of tourists filling the streets on a Sunday morning and there was no way to watch my bike had I ridden down to see the castle or take the tour. Besides, I couldn't afford the price of admission anyway whatever it was. Years later while living in the U.K., I did take the tour and loved seeing the history, architecture and grandeur that is Windsor Castle - and it was well worth it!

~~~~~~~~~~

Farnham Common, Buckinghamshire

~~~~~~~~~~

Monday, June 18, 1979   Day 21

30 Miles | Total: 1,355 Miles

101 pounds, 30 pence | Total: 284 pounds, 13 pence

~~~~~~~~~~

I spent the night in the guest room again at Bet's, and this morning I got up around 10:00 a.m., and she prepared eggs, bacon, toast, cereal and coffee for breakfast. George came over to the house and took me to the travel agency - *Henry's* in Slough. I spent $202 on a budget Pan Am return flight to Seattle for the week of July 15-21 and another 30 pence for ice cream.

I spent the afternoon around the house with Bet and walked the dogs with her in the woods. Later Ian came home and we had dinner - which was spaghetti, gin and tonics, and chocolate baked dessert. Tomorrow I'll ride on to Marny's house in Berkhamstead.

~~~~~~~~~~

2018 Editorial Comment: It was nice to be back at Bet's house, as everyone had always been so nice to me there and everything was so familiar, just like family. I knew this was a very special time in my life with what I was experiencing in the British Isles, but I couldn't know at the time it would be only the first stop on the island for what would later turn out to be years of my life here in the U.K., only under far different conditions while serving in the United States Air Force.

I knew I was running low on funds and had to make a reservation home on Pan Am so I wouldn't run out of money completely before purchasing my ticket. I didn't keep a running total in my logbook of how much money I had remaining, until it got closer to my departure date when I'd be counting my pennies while still determined to see as much of the British Isles as I could. The problem was I had almost a month yet before my flight home. I needed to balance what I could see versus how much money I had left, and not run out of either before running out of both at the same time - a delicate situation indeed.

My plan was to head towards Scotland next, but I wasn't sure exactly how I'd pull that off yet. My next stop was to go back to Marny's and get some advice on the best approach to make the journey. I was thinking I could take the train up to Scotland and then ride back down to London Heathrow, pacing myself along the way based on the date and the money I had left.

Also, the open return meant I didn't know if I would be flying out on the 15th or the 21st and wouldn't know until the week or so prior when they'd finalize the date and give me my seat number. I had to be back in time to be able to make the 15th if necessary, which meant I might still have a week left on my hands if my flight turned out to be on the 21st. In that case, I was thinking of heading over towards Wales for a couple of days. At least I'd already booked my ticket and now I just had to work the math.

Bet and the family had done so much for me, not only here in Farnham Common but also down in Christchurch. She'd gotten my adventure started off on the right foot the day I'd arrived, and now here again by taking me to the local travel agency to secure my flight home. I wouldn't have a lot of money once I arrived back home in Seattle, but I'd have more than a lifetime of memories to recall my time in this green and pleasant land...

~~~~~~~~~~

Chapter Ten - Farnham Common, Buckinghamshire, to Berkhamsted, Hertfordshire

~~~~~~~~~~

Tuesday, June 19, 1979   Day 22

25 Miles | Total: 1,380 Miles

0 pounds, 50 pence | Total: 284 pounds, 63 pence

~~~~~~~~~~

I woke up this morning and got up around 9:00 a.m., took a bath and had a breakfast of eggs, toast, cereal and coffee. After breakfast I said thank you and goodbye to Ian, and then after packing everything up I said thank you and goodbye as well to Bet. I then rode north up to Berkhamsted, retracing the same route again as I'd made early on in my journey.

At Marny's I spent some time lounging in the sun, wrote three letters (50 pence for stamps) and checked the train schedule for trains leaving in the morning for Scotland. Based on my return flight to the States - now scheduled for the week of July 15th - I made the plan to spend the rest of my time touring Scotland. I'll take the train up to Scotland and after touring the countryside ride back down to Heathrow on my bike.

So tomorrow it's off to Scotland and I'll have to get up early to make the train's departure time.

~~~~~~~~~~

2018 Editorial Comment: I didn't add a lot of detail in this last entry for *Part One* of my bicycle adventure through England, Scotland, Wales and France, but I'll try to fill in the gaps here. It was nice to be back at Marny's, as her house and Bet's family both in Farnham Common and Christchurch were the two places I'd spent the most time at, and they had all taken such good care of me. In addition, they both provided unique opportunities I would have never experienced otherwise, with the amazing tour of London's historic sites with David and Jayne, along with Andy's recording sessions while staying with Marny.

This entry brings a close to *Part One* of my trip and not only serves as a bookend to all I'd done in Southern England and France on this trip, but reflects such a different experience from what I'd have in Scotland. Everyone remained so very generous and hospitable to me on this adventure wherever I went in the U.K., but the flavor of my visit to Scotland would be reflected in the rugged landscapes and pouring rain I'd experience there. Yet, this second half of my journey would be just as special as the first half had been, but at the time in Berkhamsted I had no way of knowing how it would turn out.

Splitting this story into two different parts not only allows me to use my other favorite photo from this adventure for the cover of *Part Two,* but it allows me to frame each half of my journey at the logical dividing point of the trip. The lack of money remaining would be my constant focus on *Part Two,* as I reached a point of calculating the days left until my flight week home, versus the money I'd need to take the train down to London Heathrow to make my return flight if I ran into problems. Eventually, I'd not even have the train fare to London Heathrow on me anymore, leaving me with no *Plan B* to fall back on if needed.

I couldn't know what the future held, so I enjoyed my time that day at Marny's knowing it was possibly my final refuge before heading out into the great unknown, for the next day I'd be on a train heading to Glasgow, Scotland...

~~~~~~~~~~

Chapter Eleven - The Way Ahead

I had survived not only *Part One* of my bicycle adventure to England, Scotland, Wales and France, but had recovered from my excursion across the English Channel in search of sunshine that just couldn't be found. France had tested me to my limits, yet I was still standing there in Berkhamsted where I'd started off from in the direction of Oxford and Bath.

How I'd managed to stay in one piece and now be ready to tackle the second half of my adventure was really due to the hospitality of all those I'd come across on my travels who had taken me in. Without their generous assistance and hospitality, who knows how things might have turned out and what might have happened to me, let alone, if I'd be prepared now to head out again into the great unknown.

I was planning on taking the train to Glasgow, Scotland, first thing the next morning with the idea of touring Scotland before making my way back towards Berkhamsted in time to make my flight. Actually, I'd need to return in time to be back prior to the week of my open reserve ticket in order to find out exactly when I'd be flying out, and if it turned out I still had time on my hands, I'd put that time to good use touring Wales.

Scotland would test me physically and mentally through the remote ruggedness, isolation and beauty of its stark landscape and rain, in ways Southern England hadn't done. Towns would be few and far between in many areas of Scotland, leaving me with few options besides youth hostels to seek shelter in, as the farmers would no longer be so prominently located outside of villages where I could find someone to let me camp on their property. In many cases, it would feel like I was the only person around for miles and miles in the remote, wet and windswept countryside.

This alone would have been enough to separate my adventure into two parts, but a secondary theme emerged where I would be racing both the calendar and my remaining funds in an attempt to time my arrival back in Berkhamsted prior to running out of money altogether. I needed to be back just prior to the week of my departure date from London Heathrow, in case my flight was on the first day of the week I'd reserved to fly home. I was constantly balancing my funds remaining versus the cost of a train ticket back to Berkhamsted and London Heathrow if it came to that.

I'd traveled 1,380 miles so far on my adventure by bike, car and ferry, and spent 284 pounds, 63 pence to date including my final purchases in Seattle before leaving, which would have been roughly $583. So of the $1,000 I had for the adventure, I would have had about $417 dollars remaining. At the end of *Part Two* of my adventure, I determined there was between one and two hundred dollars that I'd spent on this journey that I hadn't recorded in my logbook. The gist of it being that I'd return to Berkhamsted with less than 20 pounds remaining on me in total - not a lot of margin for error.

My logbook was a very inefficient way to try to track expenses on this trip, as it required me to remember all the expenditures I'd made each day during what were often very long and challenging days, yet my single entry towards the end of the trip defined the fact that I no longer had even the train fare to London Heathrow on me at the time, which was probably 20 pounds or less from where I was at that time.

The people of Northern and Central England would turn out to treat me wonderfully in the same manner as the folks of Southern England had, and was yet another reason the people of the British Isles had endeared themselves to me for a lifetime! I would much later on be stationed in England with my family on two separate occasions while serving in the United States Air Force, and it was an absolute privilege, honor and highlight of my life to serve while stationed in the U.K.

I'd find out after returning from Scotland that I still had a few available days remaining to tour Wales which was a real blessing at the time, as I found parts of Wales to be almost magical in their beauty. One valley in particular seemed to pull me back in time, as if time actually stood still there. I really enjoyed both the beauty of the countryside and the people of Wales, and was entranced by their warmth, hospitality and the pure magic of their language - like visiting elves! I would later on use obscure Welsh village names and variations to populate many of the names and locations within the world of my adventure trilogy *Jonathan's Amazing Adventures* as a personal tribute to Wales and my visit there.

I was celebrating both sides of my heritage during this second part of my journey, as on my mother's side I'm Scottish with the last name of Armstrong, and on my father's side I'm of both Welsh and Central English heritage with the last name of Jones - along with a good portion of German lineage mixed in at the same time. In addition, I've voluntarily adopted both Irish and Italian heritages just out of sheer appreciation for everything they represent!

I went on to finish this entire adventure in one piece, having spent less time overseas than I'd originally imagined I would for lack of funds to continue on, while at the same time knowing that I'd made a good go of it. I was not only satisfied with my efforts, but ready to fly back across the pond to Seattle and sort out the rest of my life following the second half of my journey.

I had no way of knowing what awaited me on my return to the Pacific Northwest, but had little time to fixate on the precariousness of my situation back in the Emerald City. I was basking in the feeling of accomplishment I had in completing my first overseas adventure and wanted to spend some time recovering from the weariness of my body. I was simply planning to rest up before becoming overly concerned with my follow-on situation.

It turned out I wouldn't have to wait long before being thrown into a series of back to back to back adventures that would leave my head spinning from their frequency and the unplanned nature of their arrival, sending me back out on the road again for the rest of the summer. I'd both fly back to Detroit and make a transcontinental trip by Greyhound bus from Seattle to New York City, to drive brand new cars back across the country to Seattle, and spend two weeks in Puerto Rico visiting and SCUBA diving with a friend I'd met by chance. I'd also drive a new car from South Florida along the Gulf Coast and back up to Seattle. I'd learn lessons through both my successes and my failures during these adventures, all the while stalling for time before deciding what I'd do next with my life.

I'd contemplated walking across Central Colorado that late summer and fall, but never managed to get to the point of making the decision to actually do it before moving to an island in Puget Sound and commuting to work in downtown Seattle by ferry. After a couple of months living on Bainbridge Island, I had a revelation to return to Michigan State University to study business, and within the span of two short phone calls I was registered for Winter Term 1980 at MSU and had a room in a house reserved for me off-campus. All I had to do was mail the few boxes of personal belongings I had left back to the house in E. Lansing that I'd be living in and I was ready to take yet another Greyhound Bus - my third long-distance bus ride of the year - back to E. Lansing.

My return to Michigan State University would be interesting in four different ways. The first was that I finally cracked the code on how to study to my best advantage, based on my personal ability to learn and recall information, along with tried and true methods of learning new material. Using this method allowed me to 4.0 most of my business school courses over the following year and a half I was there at MSU on a year round basis.

The second discovery of mine on campus was finding the College of Music through serendipity when I had no realization I was even looking for it, and ventured into the basement hallway to see rooms and rooms of unused piano practice rooms which I'd put to good use doing my quest to relearn how to play the piano from an organic sense of first making friends with the instrument. This would be a journey within this college adventure that would help prepare me to begin writing my own songs years later during Advent 1989.

The third discovery of mine during spring break 1980, was squeezing in a wonderful little bicycle adventure through the idyllic countryside of Ontario, Canada. I wanted to nurture my spirit of adventure while I was back at college and had never been to Toronto before, so I bicycled from Grand Blanc, to Port Huron, MI, before crossing into Sarnia and deep into the Province of

Ontario, Canada. I fell short of my desire to reach Toronto due to cold, windy and rainy weather, but in the end had a memorable time while visiting Michigan's cross-border neighbors to the east.

My fourth discovery while back at MSU, was being invited to embark on a once in a lifetime yacht cruise with my friend Jim and his family in Seattle from Everett, WA, to Princess Louisa Inlet and Chatterbox Falls, British Columbia, Canada, and all points in-between. This turned out to be a fabulous adventure that I'm forever appreciative of for being invited along - what an experience!

I'd also learned the lesson from my very first bicycle adventure around the United States and my many travels since, to always bring a logbook or a yellow legal pad with me on every subsequent adventure I took in the years leading up to my joining the United States Air Force to fly jets as a navigator following college. This habit led to my later becoming a novelist and writer well beyond the scope of my serialized autobiography. In 2019 I'll begin preparing my first novel for publishing, with nine others to follow that are either completed or well on their way towards completion, as well as three separate full-length children's books and a motivational self-help book ready to go.

There were many other discoveries I made during my years back in college, including those of the heart and the spirit of being back in college. My biggest decision during this time of my life was again forged in the fire of failure, as I then made the decision to follow my heart and childhood dreams to fly jets as a navigator in the United States Air Force over the course of a twenty year career. I'd go on to meet my future wife, start a family, live overseas, and travel and see much of the world, and will address this chapter of my life once I've completed all the other literary projects I've started over the years.

I've been very fortunate over the course of the past 62 years of my life so far to live many of my hopes, dreams, passions and desires in life, and I hope that in sharing my journey with you, the readers, I can inspire you in some small way to live yours as well. While I never did become the veterinarian I'd hoped to have become in my youth, I did become a different kind of vet - a military veteran of the United States Air Force having served in the Cold War and the Persian Gulf War.

I've found that you need to keep placing one foot in front of the other in a continuous process of trying to strive forward in life and if you do, you'll find you've traveled quite a way down life's path once you pause for a moment to look back over your shoulder. My life has been such a series of individual chapters, that at first glance appear to be unique and set apart from the others, but in 1994 I realized they were all interconnected in ways I hadn't been able to see before.

To have arrived where I was in 1994 with my wife and son, meant I had to have traveled all the winding paths in life I'd traveled down, had to experience all the successes and failures of my life, undertaken and embarked on all the adventures I'd gone on, otherwise I wouldn't have been the person I was then, nor would I have had the family I had. Everything I'd been through at that point had been required for me to have arrived at that point in time to see in the New Year 1994 and to make my New Year's Resolution to begin writing my autobiography. In that moment my entire life seemed to make sense to me.

The same can be said for the entirety of the 24 years since beginning my autobiography in 1994 to reach this point in my life to begin self-publishing it along with all the other books I've written to date. In order to have arrived at this point in the year 2018, I had to go through the entire literary process of writing, drafting, blogging and editing to finally begin publishing my work which I'd though would always elude me. I never thought I'd be able to self-publish my stories and believed I'd need to throw myself on the mercy of a publishing company to finally make that happen - but instead, Amazon has provided me with the most amazing and life-altering opportunity to actually publish my books myself - and for that I'll be forever grateful!

There is nothing worse for a writer and an author than to have their stories remain untold within them, scattered across various sheets and stacks of paper, hidden away in binders and saved within miscellaneous thumb drives around the house without ever seeing the light of day within the pages of a published book. For a writer must write and an author must publish, and without the opportunity to have a reader visit the worlds of their stories, there is no fulfillment.

So this opportunity to self-publish has given me new life as I enter my golden years, and I aim to keep writing and publishing as long as I'm fortunate enough to be blessed with the opportunity to bring you, the readers, more stories! For you are the wind beneath my wings and the reason I'm able to continue living my dreams of writing and publishing! Thank you for reading the stories of my early adventures in life and I hope to keep you in new reading material for many years to come, as I work to self-publish the many stories I've written in draft over the past years and decades of my life!

Cheers!

Mark

~~~~~~~~~~

About the Author - Mark D. Jones

Thank you very much for reading *In Search of the Meaning of Life - Book Nine: England, Scotland, Wales & France (Part One).* After a lifetime of writing and adventuring, I'm now retired and enjoy spending my days preparing manuscripts of my writings and stories for self-publishing on Amazon.

I've lived an adventurous life and through my books I try to pass on to you my thoughts, insights, lessons learned, adventures and experiences so that you, too, can live your hopes, dreams, passions and desires in life - and adventure provides the perspective and vehicle to take you there!

You can also find me online at the following sites:

- WordPress as livelovethinkexist and Mark D. Jones

- My Author Page and Blog: *In Search of the Meaning of Life (An Autobiography)*

  https://insearchofthemeaningoflife.com/

- Twitter as @livelovethinkex and Mark D. Jones

- Facebook as Mark D. Jones

- LinkedIn as Mark D. Jones

- Google Plus as Mark D. Jones

- Amazon as Author Mark D. Jones

- Goodreads as Author Mark D. Jones

- Soundcloud as Mark Jones 104

I wish you all the very best on your adventures in life, for your heart knows the direction of your heart's desires and all you have to do is find the courage to follow it!

Bon voyage and best wishes always to you and yours for the journey and adventure of a lifetime!

Cheers!

Mark

~~~~~~~~~~

99069057R00083

Made in the USA
Columbia, SC
05 July 2018